JOHN

WESLEY BIBLE STUDIES

wphonline.com

CONTENTS

INTRODUCTION
Sonlight

Darkness settles for a long time at the North Pole, where the sun doesn't rise from late September until mid-March. But darkness rested upon Israel even longer. For four hundred years, from the prophecy of Malachi to the appearance of John the Baptist, spiritual darkness enveloped Israel. The period is called "the Silent Years," because during this time there was no prophetic communication between God and His people.

TWO MEN NAMED JOHN

But suddenly God broke His silence. He sent John the Baptist to call Israel to repent. God's Son, the Light of the World, would soon shine in the darkness. John confessed he was not the light, but was only "a witness to the light" (John 1:8).

Although God sent John the Baptist to prepare the way of the Lord, He chose John, the Beloved Apostle, to write the gospel of John. John structured his gospel around several of Jesus' miracles. The reason was to show conclusively that Jesus is "the Christ, the Son of God" and to draw the readers to faith in Jesus. All who believe in Jesus, the Son of God, receive eternal life (see John 1:12; 3:14–16; 20:30–31).

MINISTRY OF LIGHT

Wherever Jesus went, He beamed light into darkened souls — whether it was Nicodemus, a learned Pharisee who came to Him by night, or an ostracized Samaritan woman with a bad reputation, or the men who became His disciples. He spoke about the new birth; promised living water in response to faith; and identified himself as the Light of the World; the Door; the way, the truth, and the life; and the resurrection.

MORE THAN WORDS

But Jesus supported His words with actions. He healed a man who had been paralyzed thirty-eight years. He gave sight to a man who had been blind from birth. He brought Lazarus to life after he had been dead four days. John's gospel reports even more amazing actions than these, but space does not allow this study to examine all the wonders Jesus performed.

THE OLD RUGGED CROSS

Without a doubt, the clearest demonstration of Jesus' assault on darkness took place at the cross. There Jesus, the Light of the World, hung in darkness, bearing the penalty of our sins so we would not be left in darkness. Then, three days later, the clearest demonstration of His sonship took place: He arose and left an empty tomb. As it says in Romans 1:4, "And who through the Spirit of holiness was declared with power to be the Son of God by his resurrection from the dead."

SHINING THE LIGHT

As we study John's gospel, our love of Jesus will grow, and our desire to share the good news will swell. Of course, some will spurn our message, for people prefer darkness to light because their deeds are evil (John 3:19), but others may embrace it gladly. Those who believe in the Son of God will be able to say, as the healed blind man did, "I was blind but now I see" (John 9:25).

INCARNATION AND SALVATION

John 1:1–18

The incarnation gave humanity the opportunity to
know Christ and receive Him as Savior.

You will be hard-pressed to find someone willing to seriously criticize or even say anything negative about the man Jesus of Nazareth. He is almost universally admired, praised, and put forth as an example. The problem comes when you try to push the issue of His true identity. Was He just a man or something more? "He was a good man, even great," people will say, "but the Son of God? I don't go along with that."

The first chapter of the gospel of John proclaims that Jesus is the eternal Word who created all things and came to earth to provide eternal life to all who believe in Him. This study will inspire you to herald the good news of Jesus' incarnation and power to save.

COMMENTARY

John 1:1–18 is often called the prologue to John's gospel. It tells us who Jesus is so that we can fully grasp the rest of the gospel. We learn that He is the eternal Word of God who became a human being. Bible scholars use the word *incarnation* to describe this event. We are told He became human so we can receive the grace and truth (v. 17) of salvation. These verses also tell us about the world's response to Him. The purpose of the gospel of John is to encourage us to respond in faith (20:31). John 1:1–5 tell us who the eternal Word of God is and what He does. Verses 6–8 clarify the Word of God by contrasting Him with John the Baptist. The relationship of the Word to the world is described in verses 9–13 and to those of us who believe in verses 14–18. Verse 14 is crucial—the Word became a human being. Verse 18 brings the whole to a conclusion.

The Word and God (John 1:1–5)

This passage describes the deity of the Word (vv. 1–2) and His divine functions as agent of creation, source of life, and revealer of light to the world (vv. 3–5).

WORDS FROM WESLEY

John 1:1

In the beginning—(Referring to Gen. 1:1 and Prov. 8:23.) When all things began to be made by the word: In the beginning of heaven and earth, and this whole frame of created beings, the Word existed, without any beginning. He was when all things began to be, whatsoever had a beginning. *The Word*—He is *the Word* whom the Father begat or *spoke* from eternity; by whom the Father *speaking* maketh all things; who speaketh the Father to us. We have, in the eighteenth verse, both a real description of the Word, and the reason why He is so called. *He is the only begotten Son of the Father, who is in the bosom of the Father, and hath declared him. And the word was with God*—Therefore distinct from God the Father. The word rendered *with*, denotes a perpetual tendency as it were of the Son to the Father, in unity of essence. He was *with* God alone; because nothing beside God had then any being. *And the Word was God*—Supreme, eternal, independent. (ENNT)

In the beginning (v. 1). This phrase reminds us of the creation account in Genesis 1. At the time of creation, the Word already existed. What did John's first readers think he meant by "the Word"? They probably remembered that God created by His word; He spoke and things came into being. They may also have remembered that God revealed himself through the prophets by His word. In Greek, the term translated *word* could also mean the principle of order and rationality in the universe. John probably meant all of this and more. **The Word** (v. 1) is more than something God says, more than the principle of order in the world. The Word is a Person who is the complete and perfect expression of God. Few statements are more carefully crafted in Greek than the phrase **the Word was God** (v. 1). This sentence cannot accurately be translated "the Word was a god," as if the Word were something less than God. Nor can it be translated "God was the Word," as if God and the Word were totally identical. No, the Word is fully God—He is deity. And yet, **the Word** is also **with God** the Father (v. 1). These verses provide an important building block for the doctrine of the Trinity.

WORDS FROM WESLEY

John 1:4

In him was life—He was the foundation of life to every living thing, as well as of being to all that is. *And the life was the light of men.* He who is essential life, and the giver of life to all that liveth, was also the light of men; the fountain of wisdom, holiness, and happiness, to man in his original state. (ENNT)

How important it is to recognize the full deity of the Word. If He is not truly God, then He cannot bring the final revelation of God. Nor can He be our Savior. Who is the Creator, the Source of life, the Revealer of truth? God is. Yet verses 3–5 describe the Word as doing all of these things. He is the agent **through** whom **all things were made** (v. 3). He himself was not "made," because **without him nothing was made that has been made**. No one but God can have life (v. 4) in himself (compare 5:26). Yet in the Word **was life** (1:4). **Life** is a very important term in John's gospel. John was not speaking merely of physical life. He was speaking of eternal life, the very life of God. It is this life

that is the light of men and women. The life of God in the Word
enlightens human beings with God's truth.

We have learned about God through the world created by His
word and through the prophets inspired by His word. But now,
the very Word of God, the complete expression of God, has come
to reveal Him in His fullness. Many are under the control of **the
darkness** (v. 5) of sin, disobedience, and, above all, their refusal
to believe. This darkness and those controlled by it are not able
to truly understand the truth of God. Neither are they able to
overcome (v. 5, NIV footnote) or master the light. They cannot
stop the light from achieving God's purpose. Verses 9–13 give
more detail about what happened when the light of God came
into the world.

The Word and John the Baptist (John 1:6–8)

Verses 6–8 may seem to interrupt the flow of this passage,
but they are very important. The John of verse 6 is John the Baptist (compare vv. 15, 19–33) not John the apostle. He is this
gospel's first **witness** to the light revealed by the Word (v. 7).
And indeed, the whole gospel is such a witness (see 20:31;
21:24–25). But these verses also clarify the identity of the Word
by contrasting the human nature and origin of John with the eternal existence and saving revelation of the Word. **There came a
man** (1:6) contrasts with "in the beginning was the Word" (v. 1);
who was sent from God (v. 6) with "and the Word was with
God" (v. 1); **his name was John** (v. 6) with "and the Word was
God" (v. 1). One was a human being who came into existence
and was sent from God; the other always existed, was with God
always, and was, in fact, deity. One was with God in the beginning; the other came as a witness. One was the Creator; the other
was to lead people to faith in the Creator. One had the life that
was the light; the other was not the light. In one, the Light shone
in the darkness; the other was a witness to that shining.

The Word and the World (John 1:9–13)

Verse 9 picks up the theme of verse 5. The Word is the true light of God through which the life of God shines into the world. We are told that He **gives light to every man**—every human being (v. 9). This verse may indicate that the Word of God through nature and conscience gives some knowledge of God to every individual. But it is probably referring primarily to the incarnate Word of God. The incarnate Word brings God's light for everyone—not just for a few.

The term **world** (v. 9) can have several different but related meanings in John's gospel. It can mean the universe God has created. This is its primary meaning in verse 9 and in the first two occurrences in verse 10. It can also mean all human beings, or human society, often under the power of evil and in opposition to God. This is the way it is used the third time it appears in verse 10.

Verse 10 introduces the surprising response of the world. **He was in the world** probably refers to God's revelation through the Word become flesh in Jesus. We have already seen that **the world was made through him** (v. 10). Since He was in the world and He made it, we would expect the world to recognize and accept Him. But the world did not recognize Him. This is not a matter of mere innocent ignorance. It is a result of the refusal to believe (9:35–41).

But John 1:11 is even more surprising: **He came to that which was his own**—to His own heritage. He came to the people God had chosen and prepared. God had made a covenant with them and promised He would send a savior. Certainly they at least should have recognized Him, but they **did not receive him** (v. 11). This language is stronger than the language used for the world. The world did not recognize Him, and they rejected Him. Verse 12 contrasts with verses 10–11. There were some **who received him**. What did it mean to receive Him? These are **those who believed in his name** (v. 12). This phrase means much more than mental assent to Jesus as the Son of God. It describes the kind of complete trust in and commitment to Him that leads to an obedient life and that brings eternal life (see 3:16).

WORDS FROM WESLEY

John 1:14

The whole verse might be paraphrased thus; *And* in order to raise us to this dignity and happiness, *the* eternal *word*, by a most amazing condescension, *was made flesh*, united himself to our miserable nature, with all its innocent infirmities. *And* He did not make us a transient visit, but *tabernacled among us* on earth, displaying his glory in a more eminent manner, than even of old in the tabernacle of Moses. *And we*, who are now recording these things, *beheld his glory* with so strict an attention, that we can testify, it was in every respect such a glory, as became the *only begotten of the Father*. For it shone forth not only in His transfiguration, and in His continual miracles, but in all His tempers, ministrations, and conduct through the whole series of His life. In all He appeared *full of grace and truth:* He was himself most benevolent and upright; made those ample discoveries of pardon to sinners, which the Mosaic dispensation could not do: And really exhibited the most substantial blessings, whereas that was but *a shadow of good things to come.* (ENNT)

What a great privilege God gives to those who believe! He gives them **the right to become children of God** (v. 12). Unless God gave it, they could never have this right and privilege. Verse 13 describes more fully what this means. This is not a physical birth brought about by **human decision or a husband's will**. This is a birth brought about by God himself. He begets His own eternal life in those who believe so that are **born of God**. He gives them His life. They begin to live according to His nature. The themes of being born again to eternal life and becoming children of God fit together perfectly. Thus those who are born of God and have God's own life and likeness in them cannot possibly continue to live a life of sin (1 John 2:28—3:10). John was careful, however, to protect the distinction between us as the children of God and Jesus as the Son of God. We become children of God only by believing in the One who is the eternal Son of God. John even used two different Greek words: one to refer to Jesus as the Son of God and another to refer to us as the children of God.

The Word and "Us" (John 1:14–18)

In these verses, John made clear that he was talking about a real incarnation. He described with great clarity the blessings that incarnation brings to us (v. 14), to those of us who believe. **The Word became flesh** (v. 14). The eternal Word of God became a true, living, breathing human being. By making **his dwelling among us**, He lived a true human life. The Greek words used here would have reminded John's readers of God dwelling in the tabernacle or temple of the Old Testament. God once dwelt in a building. But at one time and in one place in Palestine, He dwelt in a human being, Jesus Christ. The glory, the very nature of God, was seen in Him. He was **the One and Only** (v. 14)—there was, is, and will be no one else like Him, for He and He alone has come from the Father. The glory of God shone through His whole life. But it shone in its brightest fullness in His crucifixion. He and He alone is **full of grace and truth** (v. 14). God is faithful to bring the fullness of His promised blessings of eternal life in the Son.

In tight succession, verses 15–18 give argument for the supremacy of the Word become flesh. There is the witness of John the Baptist (v. 15), the experience of believers (v. 16), and comparison with Moses (v. 17). Verse 18 brings all to conclusion.

We have already been told that John's role was as witness to the Word (vv. 6–8). What witness did John give? He gave witness to the eternal nature of the One who became flesh. As far as others could see, John was born as a human being and then Jesus was born as a human being. John was Jesus' senior. But

John declared that Jesus far **surpassed** (v. 15) him because Jesus existed as the eternal Word of God from all eternity. He was before John ever came into being. Then comes the witness of believers (v. 16). We have received greater spiritual blessing than we could imagine because in Him is the fullness of God's grace. God's grace is inexhaustible. God's saving goodness in Him brings us the privilege of being God's children, of having God dwell within us, giving us His eternal life.

The contrast in verse 17 between Moses and Jesus Christ is striking. Moses was the greatest revealer of God in the Old Testament. The law of God itself had been given through him. All else was based on this law. The law was seen as an expression of the grace and truth of God. Yet God's grace and truth came into their fullness only in Jesus Christ. An implied contrast with Moses continues in verse 18. As much as was possible for a human being, Moses had seen God (Ex. 23:10, 21–23). No one could fully see Him (Ex. 23:20). Now, however, we have One who has not only seen Him, but is qualified to give a complete revelation of Him. This One is God, the one and only. The NIV follows a better reading here by using the word **God** instead of *Son*, as many other versions do (John 1:18). This One has become flesh, a human person, and yet He is truly God. There is no one else like Him; He is in the most intimate communion with the Father. Thus, He alone can reveal God and can bring us the grace and truth of salvation.

●

WORDS FROM WESLEY

John 1:18

No man hath seen God—With bodily eyes: yet believers see Him with the eye of faith. *Who is in the bosom of the Father*—The expression denotes the highest unity, and the most intimate knowledge. (ENNT)

DISCUSSION

Jesus' nativity is more than a heartwarming story about the birth of a baby; it's about God becoming one of us so that He could redeem us.

1. What do you learn from John 1:1–5 that affirms Jesus' deity?

2. How does John refute the theory that all life is the product of chance and the survival of the fittest?

3. How does knowing Jesus created everything affect the value you place on human life?

4. Do you see any pro-life support in John 1:3? If so, what is it?

5. Why would you agree or disagree that darkness and dying aptly describe the world we live in? What contrasting qualities did Jesus bring to us by becoming a human being and dying for us?

6. What does it mean to you personally to be born of God (John 1:12)?

7. John beheld Jesus' glory. What event in particular do you think he might have been thinking about as he wrote this statement (see Matt. 17:1–8)?

8. What admirable characteristic did John the Baptist display, according to verse 17? How can you display this characteristic as you share the good news of Jesus with others?

PRAYER

Lord, we are sorry for the times when we have not recognized You and received You in our lives. Thank You for taking on flesh and dwelling among us so we can see the light and be drawn out of darkness.

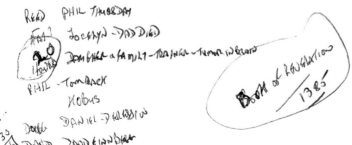

2

SPIRITUAL BIRTH

John 3:1–21

Everyone needs to experience the new birth
provided for us by God in Jesus Christ.

Have you ever heard someone say, "I wish I had my life to live all over again"? Of course, no one can become a newborn baby again and relive squandered years, but it is possible to be born again. Jesus told Nicodemus, a member of the Jewish ruling council, that it was just what he needed.

This study clears up a mystery—how to be born again when it is impossible to be born again. You will appreciate the candor and wisdom Jesus expressed when He told Nicodemus how to be born again.

COMMENTARY

This study focuses on a conversation between Jesus and Nicodemus, who "was a man of the Pharisees . . . [and] a member of the Jewish ruling council" (John 3:1). It contains Jesus' clearest teaching about the new birth, that is, being born again.

John 2 records the miracle at the wedding at Cana in Galilee and ends with an account of Jesus' cleansing the temple during the feast of Passover.

John tells us that the Jews, meaning the Jewish leaders, were indignant at the cleansing of the temple (2:18). Members of the ruling council may very well have been part of the group that questioned Jesus' authority. Certainly they would have known of the disturbance Jesus' actions caused. As a member of that council, Nicodemus came to Jesus in spite of the controversy, demonstrating that not all the Jewish leaders were opposed to Jesus' teachings. That he came to Jesus by night also probably shows Nicodemus was taking action many would have questioned. (On the other hand, a note in the NIV Study Bible suggests the timing may have been designed simply to allow for a longer conversation than would have been possible during the daytime.)

John recorded that Nicodemus was one of the few Jewish leaders who occasionally assisted Jesus. In 7:50, John wrote that Nicodemus defended Jesus before the chief priests and Pharisees, and in 19:38–40, we are told that Nicodemus assisted Joseph of Arimathea when he placed Jesus' body in the tomb. In this study, Nicodemus is shown in his nighttime encounter with Jesus, after which Nicodemus evidently became a believer. At the end of chapter 3 and following this encounter, John turned to John the Baptist, quoting his words of affirmation about Jesus: "He must become greater; I must become less" (3:30).

John's purpose in writing is stated in 20:31. It is to encourage believers to continue in their faith and also to persuade unbelievers to come to "believe that Jesus is the Christ." Throughout his gospel, John did his inspired best to present a picture of Jesus that would encourage confidence and faith.

A Man of the Pharisees (John 3:1)

Nicodemus is introduced as a **man of the Pharisees** (v. 1). Jesus often had words of condemnation for the Pharisees, because many of them were hypocritical (see Matt. 15:3–9; 23:2–7; Luke 11:39–44). They were very legalistic, following the teachings of the rabbis as well as the law of Moses and depending on their works for salvation. In contrast to the Sadducees, the Pharisees were more religious and careful to observe the traditions of the Jews. The Sadducees were more progressive and cooperated more fully with the Roman rulers. Many scholars today believe the Pharisees were the traditionalists who, by resisting outside pressure, succeeded in preserving the Jewish traditions later recorded in the Talmud. Without the Pharisees, the Jewish religion might have been absorbed and diluted into oblivion.

Nicodemus was also **a member of the Jewish ruling council** (John 1:1). The **ruling council**, or Sanhedrin, was largely made up of Sadducees, so, as a Pharisee, Nicodemus was a minority member. Under the Romans, the Sanhedrin was the Jewish body with responsibility for both religious and political policies. Nicodemus held an important position of leadership for the Jews.

You Must Be Born Again (John 3:2–8)

Whatever Nicodemus's reasons for coming to Jesus by night, he had been impressed by the miracles (or **signs** as John called them, v. 2) Jesus had already done. He simply opened with a statement of affirmation: **"We know you are a teacher who has come from God. For no one could perform the miraculous signs you are doing if God were not with him"** (v. 2).

Apparently Nicodemus was seeking for truth, but he still had a spiritual need. He did not know what to ask for, so he affirmed what he had seen Jesus do.

Jesus saw and knew Nicodemus's need, however, and came directly to the point: **"No one can see the kingdom of God unless he is born again"** (v. 3). Nicodemus took this statement in its earthly sense and was even more puzzled by it. Obviously a full-grown man or woman cannot reenter a mother's womb and be born a second time. Using common earthly analogies is helpful for understanding spiritual truths, but language falls short when it is used to describe great spiritual mysteries such as regeneration. Spiritual insight must supplement the words in order for seekers to understand. Persuasion and argument may help a person to understand, but the work of the Holy Spirit to open our minds and reveal spiritual truth is always essential.

WORDS FROM WESLEY

John 3:3

Jesus answered—That knowledge will not avail thee unless thou *be born again*—Otherwise thou canst not see, that is, experience and enjoy, either the inward or the glorious kingdom of God.

In this solemn discourse, our Lord shows, that no external profession, no ceremonial ordinances or privileges of birth, could entitle any to the blessings of the Messiah's kingdom: that an entire change of heart as well as of life, was necessary for that purpose: that this could only be wrought in man, by the almighty power of God: that every man born into the world, was by nature in a state of sin, condemnation, and misery: that the free mercy of God had gives His Son to deliver them from it, and to raise them to a blessed immortality: that all mankind, Gentiles as well as Jews, might share in these benefits, procured by His being lifted up on the cross, and to be received by faith in Him: But that, if they rejected Him, their eternal, aggravated condemnation would be the certain consequence. *Except a man be born again*—If our Lord by being *born again* means only reformation of life, instead of making any new discovery, He has only thrown a great deal of obscurity, on what was before plain and obvious. (ENNT)

Jesus continued: **"No one can enter the kingdom of God unless he is born of water and the Spirit"** (v. 5). Here, water may symbolize baptism and also purification. John the Baptist and Jesus and His disciples were probably already known for administering baptism for repentance. Many people would have also been acquainted with the practice of self-baptism by Gentile proselytes to Judaism. Baptism symbolized repentance and purification from past sins, which Nicodemus would probably understand either immediately or upon reflection.

But this new birth was more than being renewed through baptism; furthermore, it was more than a human act of purification. It was a birth of the divine Spirit. **Flesh gives birth to flesh, but the Spirit gives birth to spirit** (v. 6, compare 1:12–13). Nicodemus may not have understood fully, but he certainly was hearing new concepts about the spiritual life. Spiritual birth comes not through works, but through the gracious action of the Spirit of God.

Jesus went on: **"You should not be surprised at my saying, 'You must be born again'"** (3:7). But Nicodemus was surprised, as his statement in verse 9 demonstrates. These were new concepts he would, no doubt, ponder many times, eventually passing them on to John, who recorded them for all to read.

WORDS FROM WESLEY
John 3:7

Ye must be born again—To be born again, is to be inwardly changed from all sinfulness to all holiness. It is fitly so called, because as great as change then passes on the soul, as passes on the body, when it is born into the world. (ENNT)

Jesus continued this lesson on spiritual things: **"The wind blows wherever it pleases. You hear its sound, but you cannot tell where it comes from or where it is going. So it is with everyone born of the Spirit"** (v. 8). Nicodemus could not see or understand the wind, but he was certainly aware of its effects. Neither could he understand the mystery of the work of the divine Spirit.

The Spirit is not controlled by human choice, but acts according to His own purposes. His power, actions, and timing are under His own sovereign control. With limited insight, we humans do not fully understand or control the wind, nor do we understand or control the working of the Spirit. But we who have been born again are certainly aware of the Spirit's working; it is just as real to us as the wind.

Earthly and Heavenly Things (John 3:9–15)

Understandably, Nicodemus was puzzled by Jesus' teaching. Assuming he was sincere, he was open to new insights, but his understanding had to catch up. Verse 10 may be a rebuke by Jesus, or it might even be considered as an example of Jesus' humor. **"You are Israel's teacher . . . and do you not understand these things?"** (v. 10). Often, we who are teachers think we know far more than we do. We may take ourselves and the finality of our teaching too seriously. We have so much to learn from Jesus and His words to us. He not only tells the truth (v. 11), He is **the truth** (14:6).

Nicodemus had already affirmed that Jesus was a teacher who had come from God. Jesus built on that affirmation: **"I tell you the truth, we speak of what we know, and we testify to what we have seen"** (3:11). If Nicodemus really believed Jesus was a teacher from God, then he should have demonstrated that belief in response to Jesus' words. **"I have spoken to you of earthly things and you do not believe; how then will you believe if I speak of heavenly things? No one has ever gone into heaven except the one who came from heaven—the Son of Man"** (vv. 12–13). Jesus claimed heavenly access to and knowledge of God. No doubt Nicodemus was hearing far more than he had anticipated when he came to Jesus. But Jesus was stating deep spiritual truths for this seeker. Truth is of God; truth is in the words of Jesus. It was up to Nicodemus to choose to believe.

Jesus then illustrated the decision facing Nicodemus and all humankind: **"Just as Moses lifted up the snake in the desert, so the Son of Man must be lifted up, that everyone who believes in him may have eternal life"** (vv. 14–15). In the desert, the Israelites could look at the snake and their physical lives would be preserved (see Num. 21:8–9). Surely, none of them would refuse; yet many Israelites died. Now an analogous choice was presented to the world: believe in the Son of Man and have eternal life. In contrast to the Israelites and the bronze snake, this choice had eternal significance. And this was the exact choice facing Nicodemus at that moment. But that choice was not limited to Nicodemus; it was universal in scope, extending to all humankind in all ages, even the present.

God So Loved the World (John 3:16–18)

Jesus continued His message of hope for humanity. **"For God so loved the world that he gave his one and only Son, that whoever believes in him shall not perish but have eternal life"** (v. 16). Why did Christ come? Because of God's infinite love. For whom did He come? The whole world of condemned sinners — including each of us. What did He offer to us? Eternal life instead of the condemnation we deserve. How should we respond? Believe!

WORDS FROM WESLEY

John 3:16

Yea, and this was the very design of God's love, in sending Him into the world: *Whosoever believeth on him* — With that faith which worketh by love, and hold fast the beginning of His confidence steadfast to the end. *God so loved* the world — That is, all men under heaven; even those that despise His love, and will *for that cause* finally perish. Otherwise not to believe would be no sin to them. For what should they believe? Ought they to believe that Christ was given for them? Then He was given for them. *He gave his only Son* — Truly and seriously. And *the Son of God gave himself* (Gal. 4:4). Truly and seriously. (ENNT)

Recall that this wonderful message of universal hope was given to a single man, Nicodemus. Surely his mind was reeling from the scope of what he heard! It is doubtful that Nicodemus really understood the implications at that time. After years of contemplation, Paul later wrote, "O the depth of the riches and wisdom and knowledge of God! How unsearchable are his judgments and how inscrutable his ways!" (Rom. 11:33 NRSV).

Marvelously, **God did not send his Son into the world to condemn the world, but to save the world** from the condemnation we deserve (John 3:17). And that salvation is offered to everyone who believes (v. 18). But those who do not believe remain under condemnation for their sins and especially for the greatest sin of all—refusing to believe in God's only Son (v. 18). Nicodemus had a hard time believing earthly things, and Jesus was giving him an extensive lesson in heavenly things as well. Much about this wonderful insight into the plan and purpose of God remains shrouded in mystery. We can never understand fully, but, as Isaac Watts wrote, "Love so amazing, so divine, demands my life, my soul, my all."

Light and Darkness (John 3:19–21)

John 1:4–9 discusses the theme of light and darkness. Here, John continued that theme and discussed why some come to the light and others turn away. **Light has come into the world, but men loved darkness instead of light because their deeds were evil** (v. 19). Light exposes both evil and truth (vv. 20–21). Those who believe come to the light because their deeds are forgiven. Their love for evil has been broken by the grace and power of God through the cross. Those who refuse to repent (that is, turn from their evil ways) try to hide in the darkness so their deeds will not be known. Sadly, they continue in slavery to their evil ways.

Jesus' message to Nicodemus, to all of us: Respond to God's love, turn from the darkness, turn to the light, and believe!

WORDS FROM WESLEY
John 3:21

He that practiseth the truth (that is, true religion) *cometh to the light*—So even Nicodemus afterward did. *Are wrought in God*—That is, in the light, power, and love of God. (ENNT)

DISCUSSION

When Jesus spoke to Nicodemus about being born again, He was giving him the opportunity to experience God's new creation.

1. Why do you think Nicodemus came to Jesus at night instead of during the day? *[handwritten: NEED MORE TIME]*

[handwritten left margin: SEEKING TRUTH / PHARISEE / SECRET]

2. What convinced Nicodemus that Jesus was a teacher who had come from God? *[handwritten: MIRACULOUS SIGNS ONLY FROM GOD]*

3. What is your general impression of the Pharisees? Why do you agree or disagree that a form of Pharisaism exists today? *[handwritten: CLOSELY FOLLOW TRADITIONS]*

[handwritten left margin: HYPOCRITICAL / LEGALISTIC / FOCUSED ON LAW]

4. How can you help a religious person see his or her need to be born again? *[handwritten: SPIRITUAL INSIGHT MUST SUPPLEMENT WORDS / TO DEMONSTRATE DUTY TO HELP / GODS SON]*

5. Why is the wind an appropriate analogy for the ministry of the Holy Spirit? *[handwritten: FELT, SEEN but DON'T KNOW WHERE IT COMES FROM or GODS / SEE EFFECTS / REAL POWER]*

[handwritten left margin: EVERYONE with BELIEVES WILL HAVE ETERNAL LIFE]

6. If a fellow Christian asked you how he or she might gain more knowledge of spiritual truth, what advice would you give? *[handwritten: READ JOHN, PRAY ASK THE LORD SEEK, WORDS IN PLACE]*

7. How would you define *perish?* How would you define *eternal life?* *[handwritten: LIVE IN THE KINGDOM of GOD / GO TO HEAVEN / ABSENCE OF GOD]*

8. How will you show your gratitude this week for God's amazing love? *[handwritten: WITH PRAYER OF THANKS. HELP FOR CONTINUED GUIDANCE PRAY]*

PRAYER

Father, thank You for giving Your Son Jesus so we may enter Your kingdom and have eternal life with You. Help us to never take the good news of the gospel for granted. Use our actions to reflect Your light so others may believe as well.

3

MAKING EVANGELISM PERSONAL

John 4:4–26, 39

Sharing our faith in Christ with others is God's plan for
reaching the world with salvation.

Even the most ardent golfer must wonder if it's worth finishing
a round in ninety-plus-degree temperatures under a blazing sun.
Nevertheless, she keeps playing until she reaches a tee box with a
water cooler. There, she lingers to enjoy a refreshing drink of
water; and then she resumes play until burning thirst strikes again.
It seems even multiple cups of cold water can't quench her thirst
for long.

But, as this study shows, Jesus offers water that quenches thirst
forever. Discover the well of living water!

COMMENTARY

Jesus was never limited by location, social issues, or people's
personalities. He went where His Father told Him to go and did
what His Father told Him to do. This study shows how far Jesus
traveled to do this . . . all the way to Samaria—the land all Jews
avoided.

Samaria (John 4:4–6)

Now he had to go through Samaria (v. 4). Samaria separated
Judea in the south from Galilee in the north. Judea was the land
of the Jews. Many Jews also lived in Galilee, but the Jews and the
Samaritans did not get along well with one another. Most Jews
avoided going through Samaria on their way from Judea to Galilee.
They would cross to the east side of the Jordan, go north, and then

cross back into Galilee. Geography did not force Jesus to go through Samaria; He went by divine appointment.

It is instructive to contrast Jesus' time in Samaria with His time in Judea as recorded in John 2:12—3:36. Jesus had gone to the temple, the center of the Jewish faith. When He cleansed the temple, He demonstrated that He was replacing it with himself (see John 2:19–22). People would come to God through Him and not at the temple. The leaders rejected Him, or else they were unable to understand Him. But now Jesus has come to Samaria.

The Jews considered Samaritans heretics. Under David and Solomon, Israel had been one nation. At the time of Solomon's son, the nation was divided in two—Israel in the north, Judah in the south. In 722 B.C., the Assyrians carried the northern nation of Israel away into captivity. They brought many pagan peoples into mix with the remnant of Israel. This mixture of pagans and Israelites became the Samaritans. Although it had been destroyed by Jesus' time, the Samaritans had once had a temple on Mount Gerizim. They claimed that Mount Gerizim, not Jerusalem, was the place where God should be worshiped. After all, Abraham (Gen. 12:7) and Jacob (33:20) had built altars near this mountain. When the Israelites first entered the Promised Land, they had been blessed at Mount Gerizim (Deut. 11:29; 27:12). Gerizim was very near the city of **Sychar** (John 4:5), the site of this study. The Samaritans traced their ancestry back to Jacob (v. 6), also called Israel, considering him the father of their nation. Jacob's son Joseph had been the father of the tribes of Ephraim and Manasseh, the two largest tribes in north Israel, Samaria.

These verses, then, take place at the center of this heretic Samaritan nation, in sight of Mount Gerizim, **near the plot of ground Jacob had given to his son Joseph** (v. 5), right at the well Jacob himself had bequeathed to his children. Jesus, tired from traveling on foot up and down the dusty hills of Samaria, **sat down by** this **well . . . about the sixth hour** (v. 6), around noon.

Living Water (John 4:7–14)

At the well, Jesus addresses **a Samaritan woman** (v. 7) of ill repute. She may have been coming at noon **to draw water** because she was ashamed to come when others were there.

"Will you give me a drink?" (v. 7). It was normal to request a drink in hot, dusty Palestine. Normal, except when the request was made of a Samaritan woman by a Jewish man (v. 9). For the reasons given above, the **Jews** did **not associate with Samaritans**—they avoided them (v. 9). But Jesus quickly moved past this barrier of cultural prejudice. He came to the woman as one in need with a request for her help. He then ignored her surprise at His lack of prejudice and went straight to the crucial issue—**the gift of God** (v. 10) for her.

WORDS FROM WESLEY

John 4:7

Give me to drink—In this one conversation he brought her to that knowledge, which the apostles were so long in attaining. (ENNT)

Because of Jesus' unusual behavior and answer, the woman began to wonder **who it** was **that** asked her **for a drink** and what this **gift of God** was, this **living water** He offered (v. 10). **Living water** was a term that could refer to a flowing stream or spring, as contrasted with a stagnant pool. She saw no "flowing water." All she saw was a **deep** well and a person who had **nothing** with which **to draw** water from that well (v. 11). After all, hadn't He asked her for a drink? Their **father Jacob** had given them this **well**, even drunk **from it himself**. Was this man **greater than . . . Jacob** (v. 12)? Was He going to give them flowing water?

Again, Jesus went to the heart of the matter. He described what this living water is by telling her what it will do for her.

First of all, this water satisfies. Regular **water** (v. 13) satisfies for awhile, but the one who drinks living water will be really satisfied: he or she **will never thirst** (v. 14). This living water will keep satisfying, for it **will become . . . a spring of water welling up** within the person who receives it, producing **eternal life** (v. 14). Water is the life-producer. Where there is no water, there is no life. John 7:37–39 indicates that this living water is the Holy Spirit, whom Jesus will give to those who believe in Him. It is the indwelling presence of God that gives us eternal life. Jesus invited this Samaritan woman to come and drink and see for herself the deep and lasting satisfaction that comes from this water.

WORDS FROM WESLEY
John 4:12

Our father Jacob—So they fancied he was; whereas they were, in truth, a mixture of many nations, placed there by the king of Assyria, in the room of the Israelites whom he had carried away captive (2 Kings 17:24). *Who gave us the well*—In Joseph, their supposed forefather: *And drank thereof*—So even he had no better water than this. (ENNT)

She Who Drank the Living Water (John 4:15–18)

"Give me this water so that I won't get thirsty and have to keep coming here to draw water" (v. 15). How nice it would be not to have to do this chore of drawing water every day. It gets hard carrying enough water back for a household. She still didn't understand, but she wanted to taste for herself.

Before we can drink the living water, however, we have to admit our need, our sin. Jesus' command to **call** her **husband** (v. 16) led her to admit the sinful situation of her life. **"I have no husband"** (v. 17) was a true answer that concealed the truth. But Jesus knew and exposed the truth behind it (v. 18). When we come to

Jesus for the living water, He exposes the depths of our hearts. We must come to grips with who we are, confess our deepest need, and seek His help.

He Who Gives the Living Water (John 4:19–26, 39)

The woman saw clearly that Jesus was someone special. His unusual knowledge of her led her to believe He was a **prophet** (v. 19). The Samaritans were looking for the prophet like Moses (Deut. 18:18)—the promised Messiah or Christ. Like Moses, this prophet would be a great revealer of God's truth. Her question in John 4:19 seems like an attempt to deflect attention from her own sinful condition. But what an opportunity. If this man was the much-anticipated prophet, and yet He was a Jew, she would ask about the central issue that divided Jews and Samaritans: Was **this mountain**—Mount Gerizim—the proper place to worship God, or was the temple **in Jerusalem** (v. 20)? Her ancestors said one, and the Jews said the other.

Jesus does not get bogged down in theological debate. The question has become secondary in the light of His coming. **A time is coming** (v. 21). Jesus' ministry was bringing an end to the old era, to the time for debating the geographical location of worship. Jesus is the one who can call God Father. He is the one who fully reveals the **Father**. In John 2:19–22, Jesus showed He replaces the Jerusalem temple as the place to meet God. And since He would soon give the Holy Spirit to all who believe in Him, it would no longer be a matter of worshiping **on this mountain** or **in Jerusalem** (4:21).

Although Jesus focused on the main issue, He did answer her question. The **Samaritans** (v. 22) worshiped in ignorance. The Jews worshiped with a true knowledge of God, for it was through them that God was bringing **salvation** for all. But even deluded Samaritans can become **true worshipers** (v. 23). **A time is coming and has now come** (v. 23). In Jesus' ministry, the time was coming, and after His death and resurrection, it would fully arrive. In this time, it will not be a question of geography, but of worshiping God as **Father** and **in spirit and truth** (v. 24). It will not matter where people worship God, only how. They must worship Him as the Father of our Lord Jesus Christ, as the One who makes us His children. They must worship Him in spirit, sincerely, from the depths and integrity of their hearts. They must worship Him according to the truth revealed in Jesus His Son. God seeks this kind of worshiper because He **is spirit** (v. 24). He is not confined to any geographical location but is present to all of His children everywhere. He deals directly with their inner beings. With the coming of Jesus, God is present with His people in a new way. Jesus gives them the Spirit of God. Sincerely worshiping according to the truth and with obedience is what matters.

WORDS FROM WESLEY
John 4:24

God is a Spirit—Not only remote from the body, and all the properties of it, but likewise full of all spiritual perfections, power, wisdom, love, holiness. And our worship should be suitable to His nature. We should worship Him with the truly spiritual worship of faith, love, and holiness, animating all our tempers, thoughts, words, and actions. (ENNT)

Jesus had given the woman a true answer to her question. But He used her question to move to the most important question of all: the true worship of God.

The woman seemed to understand that receiving this living water depended not on Mount Gerizim or on Jerusalem, but on Jesus. It depends on receiving Him for who He is and trusting in Him. She had been wondering if He was the **prophet** or Messiah (v. 19). Then she said, **"I know that Messiah"** (called **Christ**) **"is coming.**

When he comes, he will explain everything to us" (v. 25). **Messiah** is the Hebrew equivalent of the Greek word **Christ**. Both words mean "anointed one" and refer to the savior the Old Testament promised God would send to bring His plan of salvation to its conclusion. Notice that it is Jesus' ability to explain everything that has impressed her.

Jesus confirmed her in her faith: **"I who speak to you am he"** (v. 26). She was ready for Jesus to openly declare who He was. And she believed!

WORDS FROM WESLEY

John 4:26

Jesus saith—Hasting to satisfy her desire before His disciples came. *I am He*—Our Lord did not speak this so plainly to the Jews who were so full of the Messiah's temporal kingdom. If He had, many would doubtless have taken up arms in His favour, and others have accused Him to the Roman governor. Yet He did in effect declare the thing, though He denied the particular title. For in a multitude of places He represented himself, both as the Son of man, and as the Son of God: both which expressions were generally understood by the Jews as peculiarly applicable to the Messiah. (ENNT)

The following verses show her running to town to invite others to believe in Him as the Christ. She left her water jar behind (v. 28). After all, what was a water jar when she had living water to tell them about! **Many** other **Samaritans** in that town believed because of this woman's testimony (v. 39). Note how impressed they were that Jesus had told her **everything** she **ever did**. When we truly come to Him, He exposes the depths of our hearts. The faith of these Samaritans did not continue to rest only in the woman's testimony. When they experienced Jesus for themselves, they believed because of their own experience of Him (v. 42). They believed He was the Savior of the world.

We are reminded of John 1:11–12. Jesus came to His own at Jerusalem in 2:12—3:36. His own did not receive Him. When He put himself in the place of the temple, they turned from Him. Even one as sincere as Nicodemus did not seem to be able to understand spiritual things. But some did receive Him—the outcast, Samaritan heretics. And the first of them was a woman of ill repute. The living Christ corrected their theology by giving them himself.

Let us sum up how Jesus approached this woman. He humbled himself in His human need by asking for a drink. He offered her living water—himself. He helped her look at her own sinfulness. He stuck to the main point—living water. He did not get distracted by arguing about lesser issues; He used the lesser issues to focus on the important. She came to faith. She came to such a faith that she immediately led many others to faith. This passage is an invitation to us. No matter if we are poor or despised by others, Jesus comes to us offering eternal life if we will confess our sinful need and put our faith in Him as the Savior of the world. Our faith must lead to a new way of life, a life of sharing Him with our friends and neighbors.

Jesus' approach to this woman is also a pattern for our own approach to others with the gospel. None are too sinful or despised by the world to receive the gospel message. Often those the world considers lowest are most ready to receive. We must come in humility, not with a sense of superiority. We must offer them Christ—the living Christ, not some easy formula or doctrine. We must help them realize their sinfulness and need to come to repentance. We must use doctrine to guide them to the living Christ. Once they have truly experienced Him, they will know Him for themselves and be able to share Him with others.

DISCUSSION

The gospel is not restricted to people of a certain background, culture, or personality type; the gospel is good news for anyone who will believe.

1. Do you think Jesus had to go through Samaria because He wanted to take the shortest possible route from Judea to Galilee? What other reason might have compelled Him to go through Samaria?

2. How would you describe your compulsion to share the good news with an unbeliever? What might you do to strengthen that compulsion?

3. Jesus refused to harbor racial prejudice. How can you reach out across racial or cultural lines to share God's love?

4. How did the Samaritan woman's opinion of Jesus mature as Jesus spoke with her?

5. Do you agree or disagree that most Christians you know are leading a life that resembles a vibrant spring of water? What might cause a believer's life to stagnate?

6. In your opinion, how are many non-Christians trying unsuccessfully to assuage their spiritual thirst?

7. How can you worship God "in spirit"? How can you worship Him "in truth"? How are these two elements of worship connected?

8. What evidence of salvation did the Samaritan woman give?

9. You may not have a conversation at a well, but how might you use a conversation at a coffee pot to share the gospel?

PRAYER

Father, open our eyes to see the unloved and outcast around us. Open our hearts to love them as You love them. Open our mouths to share the greatest love story of all, the gospel of Jesus the Messiah.

4

THE WHOLENESS OF HEALING

John 5:1–15

Jesus healed people to reveal the will of the Father
and to make people whole.

What is the longest time you've sat in a waiting room to see
a doctor or in an emergency room for treatment? Thirty minutes?
An hour? Longer? A paralyzed man lay helplessly beside a pool
of healing waters for thirty-eight years. Each year must have
seemed like an eternity as disappointment filled his soul. But
finally Jesus, the Great Physician, came to him and healed him
instantly. Suddenly, the man could get up and walk.

As you go through this study, be aware that Jesus can make
sinners whole. He can raise them up from their sin and guilt and
empower them to walk in newness of life.

COMMENTARY

This story of the invalid who was healed at the pool is one of
several John told to demonstrate what happens when a person
receives Christ in his or her life through faith. In one of the key
verses of his gospel, John stated, "To all who received him, to those
who believed in his name, he gave the right to become children
of God" (John 1:12). John explained the meaning of this statement
through the signs that follow it. Jesus changed water into wine
at the wedding feast (2:1–11). Jesus changed the temple in
Jerusalem by cleansing it (2:12–16). Jesus changed Nicodemus,
a religious leader, with a message about a personal spiritual birth
(3:1–21). Jesus changed the woman at the well, whose life had
been shattered through five divorces, by letting her drink living

water that satisfied her heart (4:1–26). Jesus changed the life of a little boy who was at death's door by healing him (4:43–53). Jesus changed Lazarus, who was dead, by raising him to life (11:17–44). When we believe and receive Christ, the power of God makes us children of God, which includes changed lives.

The miracles of Jesus, His personal ministry to people, and His cleansing of the temple indicate that when Jesus encounters people in the Gospels, He intends to change their lives.

Each of the miracles mentioned above clearly teaches this. When Jesus changed the water into wine, not only did He chemically change the ingredients of the water in the pots and the social environment caused by the insufficient quantity of supplies at that wedding party, but He also produced a genuine happiness in guests' lives that was better than any substitute. When Jesus healed the officer's son, He gave us assurance that in life's difficulties, God can change our situation. God is sufficient. When Jesus changed Lazarus, who had been dead in the tomb for four days, He demonstrated that the power of God can reach beyond our temporal life—a change that reaches beyond the grave.

Not only the miracles of Jesus, but also His personal ministry to people indicate that He came to change lives. Jesus instructed Nicodemus that our lives are to be changed by God's grace until it appears as though we have experienced the birth process again. Jesus demonstrated to the woman at the well that no matter how much baggage we carry, our lives can be changed.

Even the cleansing of the temple indicates Jesus wants to change us by cleaning the cathedral of our hearts, the place where we worship God: "The old has gone, the new has come!" (2 Cor. 5:17).

The Setting of the Healing at the Pool (John 5:1–4)

This was Jesus' second trip to Jerusalem. The law instructed the Jews to go to Jerusalem three times a year to celebrate

laws
ARM
LEGAL

Passover, Pentecost, and the fall Feast of Tabernacles (Deut. 16:16).

The location of this healing was at a **pool . . . called Bethesda.** This pool was **near the Sheep Gate** (John 5:2). **The Sheep Gate** was located on the north wall near its northeastern corner, north of the temple area. For centuries, there has been a discussion about the correct name and exact location of this pool. Among the names various texts and translations use is Bethsaida, which means, "fishing house." The Fish Gate was also located on the north wall, immediately west of the Sheep Gate. This might affirm that the location of the pool was just north of the temple area.

The name **Bethesda,** used both by the KJV and NIV, means "house of mercy." This lonely man, imprisoned by his immobility, needed mercy. He had lost any claim to position or power as well as his ability to generate wealth. Mercy was his only hope.

WORDS FROM WESLEY

John 5:2

Thur., August 6th. Tonight God shook many souls by the word of His power. My subject was the pool of Bethesda.

Coming to pray by a poor Welshwoman, she began with me, "Blessed be God that ever I heard you! Jesus, *my* Jesus, has visited me on a bed of sickness. He is in my heart. He is my strength. None shall pluck me out of His hand. I cannot leave Him, and He will not leave me." It was the spirit of her Father that spoke in her: "O, do not let me ask for death, if thou wouldst have me live. I know thou canst keep me from ever sinning more. If thou wouldst have me live, let me walk humbly with thee all my days."

I sat and heard her sing the new song, till even my hard heart was melted. She glorified the Saviour of the world, who would have all men to be saved. "I know it, I feel it," said she: "He would not have one sinner lost. Believe, and He will give you all what He hath given me." (JCW, vol. 1, 292–293)

He and his disabled friends believed that whoever first entered the pool after its surface was disturbed would be healed. They passed the time together in daily dialogue. They had the common bonds of disabilities, of desiring to be healed, and of being disappointed because they were still sick. In spite of these bonds, at the moment of potential healing, selfishness became paramount while each one worked for his own healing. Then one Sabbath day, Jesus visited Bethesda.

Jesus Meets the Invalid (John 5:5–9)

The word *invalid* comes from a negative of the verb *to strengthen*. It means to weaken. It can be applied to the physical body, the spiritual life, or moral aspects of a person. In this case, it applied to all three. Since this man's weakness affected body, soul, and spirit, mercy was appropriate.

Thirty-eight years (v. 5) is long enough for a person to give up hope, accept the inevitable, and be content with his or her situation. In spite of all of this man's efforts, he always failed to reach the pool in time. This weak man could not win the race.

Jesus asked the invalid, **"Do you want to get well?"** (v. 6). What a foolish question. Everyone desires to be well! Yet, sometimes it is desirable to remain sick. If the man did get well, then he would have to leave the shelter of Bethesda and the comfort of his friends. He would have to leave the "house of mercy," where people cared for his needs and gave him sympathy. Independence meant he would have to provide for himself and those for whom he should assume responsibility. He would have to leave his safety net.

The invalid said he did not have anyone to help him (v. 7). The feeling of isolation, abandonment, or loneliness is one of every human's greatest fears. Where was this man's family? His parents may have been too old to help him or even deceased. But where was his wife? Did he have any children, nephews, nieces, or cousins who could have helped him? Where were his friends? In all of his life, had he not endeared anyone to himself who could and would have helped him? Is it possible that the weakness that restricted him also hindered his family or friends from helping him? Is it possible that his doubt had infected the goodwill and sacrificial help of his loved ones? This man had been without aid for so long that he did not recognize help when he had it. More than putting him in the water, this new Friend would heal him.

Jesus healed the invalid. He told the man, **"Get up! Pick up your mat and walk"** (v. 8). These verbs (**get**, **pick**, and **walk**) are in the active voice. Too often, we focus our walk with God in passive verbs; we tend to merely study what God has done: He alone could provide salvation for humankind, and He alone could pay the price for our sin. Yet at some point, we must act on what God has done for us. Seeking God, repenting, confessing, expressing faith, offering restitution, and obeying are our actions made possible by and in response to what God has done for us. Faith must produce action or it is dead (James 2:17, 20, 26).

Jesus **cured** the invalid (John 5:9). His weakness was removed, and he was made strong. He got up, picked up, and walked after thirty-eight years—a miracle. This man had done what most folks would do: He had been looking for a miracle through his own efforts. But when he met Jesus, he believed in Him and obeyed what He said. The will of God became his rule.

Jesus performed this ministry on the Sabbath day, so this story gives us insight into what Jesus might have typically done that day. In addition to attending the synagogue, Jesus may have visited those who needed the grace of God. One of the ways to make the Sabbath day holy is to provide an opportunity for the power of God to meet people's needs. God then hallows that day with His presence.

Legalistic Jews Oppose the Healing (John 5:9–13)

The miracle took place on the Sabbath. Jesus solved the sick man's problem by healing him. Now, others questioned the action of Jesus. For them, it would have been better for the man to remain sick than for Jesus to heal the man on the Sabbath day. Can we negotiate a solution of the two views? No. Either we agree with Jesus that it is permissible for the power of God to heal a person on the Sabbath, or we agree with Jesus' accusers that even healing the sick broke the Sabbath laws. Do we appreciate the grace of God or do we approach life legalistically? Contrast how Jesus and the Jewish legalists observed the day. Jesus went to the "house of mercy" and showed mercy. These Jewish leaders observed the day by criticizing the good that was done.

We who have been in church for a long time sometimes tend to judge events by external standards with which we feel comfortable. Too many times, we forget the excitement of the new believer. Life's ultimate goal should be the establishment of the will and rule of God upon an individual. This man was doing what Jesus told him to do.

The Jews ask the healed man who told him to break the law (v. 12). For them, the healed life was not as important as the life that obeyed their traditions. The Law said, "Remember the Sabbath day by keeping it holy" (Ex. 20:8). Is not the manifestation of the power of God changing a life an event that would hallow the sacred day?

The man did not know who had made him whole (John 5:13). A person is not saved by knowledge, but by faith. He did not know who; he only knew what. Once he was immobile; now he could walk and carry loads.

The Change Goes Deeper Than the Surface (John 5:14–15)

Jesus told him to **stop sinning** (v. 14). Apparently, the man's captivating weakness had been related to his sin, which had affected his body, spiritual being, and moral life. His sin was at the root of his isolation from family and friends; it was the source of his doubt. His sin blinded his eyes to the possibility of a cure. One of humanity's great delusions concerns the nature of sin. It seems good, harmless, and without effect on anyone. In fact, it has devastating effects personally, socially, and spiritually.

WORDS FROM WESLEY
John 5:14

Thur., September 30th. My subject was John 5:14: "Afterward Jesus findeth him in the temple, and said unto him, Behold, thou art made whole: sin no more, lest a worse thing come unto thee." I warned them against that sweet doctrine, "Once in grace, always in grace," but not in a controversial way; pointed out some of the infinite ways, whereby they might forfeit their pardon. I exhorted them to go to church, that they might be found of Jesus in the temple; and, above all, to pray always, that that word might be written on their hearts, "Go and sin no more."

The day was well spent in making up a difference which the sower of tares had occasioned among the principal members of the Society. (JCW, vol. 2, 118)

God's answer to sin is not legalism; it is receiving the power of God through faith in Jesus Christ. Legalism is a human effort to control the behavior of others. Its focus is in history. Its nature is to bind people within certain limits. God by nature is dynamic, life-giving, and life-changing. God, who remembers His covenants and His people, is in the present tense. He is. He called himself "I AM" (Ex. 3:14).

Jesus told the new Christian to stop sinning. Some people say Christians continue to sin just as they did before they became believers. Others say Christians can't sin. Jesus is saying Christians *shouldn't* sin. Nothing hurts the Christian as much as sin does. Nothing hurts a church more than for a Christian to sin.

The power of God changed the man from his weakness to strength. Now Christ is expanding that change into the spiritual and moral dimensions of his life.

WORDS FROM WESLEY

John 5:15

The Saviour still delights to find
His patients in the house of prayer,
Shows himself good, and doubly kind
To all that humbly seek Him there.
Their souls with grace confirming meets,
Their cure continues and completes.
For Thee I in Thy temple stay,
For Thee before Thine altar lie;
Thou Lamb who bear'st my guilt away,
Wilt Thou not further sanctify,
Give always what Thou once didst give,
And in mine inmost essence live?
Tell me again that Thou hast heal'd
The worst of all the sin-sick race,
Assure me of my pardon seal'd,
Repeat the word of saving grace,
And bid me in Thy Spirit's power
Go conquering on, and sin no more.
Continual need of Thee I have
My faith to give, confirm, increase;
I sink, if Thou forbear to save
Relapse into my old disease,
Lose all my power and life and zeal,
And justly claim the fiercest hell.
But O I never, never need
Thy grace abuse and sin again,
I may from strength to strength proceed;
I shall the promised help obtain,
Retrieve the perfect health of love,
And take my place prepared above. (PW, vol. 11, 366)

Jesus strengthened the mind and will of the man (John 5:15). This man, who had been immobilized by his sin and its debilitating power until he could not effectively function in society, now stood before his critics and testified about Jesus, who healed him. The power of God can enable His children to be faithful witnesses.

WORDS FROM WESLEY

John 5:15

The man went and told the Jews, that it was Jesus who had made him whole—One might have expected, that when he had published the name of his benefactor, crowds would have thronged about Jesus, to have heard the words of His mouth, and to have received the blessings of the gospel. Instead of this, they surround Him with a hostile intent: they even conspire against His life, and for an imagined transgression in point of ceremony, would have put out this light of Israel. Let us not wonder then, if our good be evil spoken of: if even candour, benevolence, and usefulness, do not disarm the enmity of those who have been taught to prefer sacrifice to mercy; and who disrelishing the genuine gospel, naturally seek to slander and persecute the professors, but especially the defenders of it. (ENNT)

This man at the pool had been totally humbled by the effects of his sin. The Master changed him physically, spiritually, and morally by removing the crippling effects of sin and strengthening him. This man demonstrated that he was a changed individual when he got up, picked up his bed, and walked. Conversion begins by God's grace, but it also changes us and affects the various areas of our lives, so that we too function differently.

DISCUSSION

Jesus is not only interested in healing the "spiritual" part of our lives; He also wants to bring healing to our whole life and all of our relationships. *SALVATION IS JEWISH ?*
HONOUR WHAT HE MADE

1. Why were Jesus and His disciples in Jerusalem? What does this tell you about Jesus' devotion to Old Testament law?

2. Why do you think the lame man lay for thirty-eight years so close to the temple but had no one to help him?

3. Likely, a number of spiritually needy individuals and families live close to your church. How might you help them find healing for their souls? *INVITE TO CHURCH. SHARE TESTAMONY.*

4. Jesus healed the invalid on the Sabbath. What acts of mercy might you and your Christian friends perform on the Lord's Day? *RELATIONSHIP WITH JESUS OUT OF THIS HELP*

5. What might have been Jesus' reason for slipping away into the crowd after healing the lame man? *JESUS INISHIATED*

6. Why do you agree or disagree that the lame man's affliction was the result of his sinning? *JESUS SAID SIN NO MORE*

7. Do you think it is possible to endure long-term suffering for the glory of God? If so, how might a permanently disabled or ill Christian glorify God? *YES POSSIBLE - STRONG FAITH*
NICK VUKAVICS?

8. Read John 20:30–31. What was the ultimate purpose of the healing of the lame man and the other miracles Jesus performed? *LIFE IN HIS NAME.*

PRAYER

Jesus, thank You for offering healing and forgiveness. Help us to stop sinning so we can experience the wholeness only You can provide. Expose the areas of our lives that need to change as Your grace changes us.

FULFILL) PROPHETS

BE APPRECIATIVE
JESUS HAD TO DIE ON PASSOVER

(14)

5

RESPONDING TO JESUS

John 7:25–43

Your attitude about Jesus and response toward Him
have eternal consequences.

In 2010 when LeBron James chose to leave the Cleveland Cavaliers and sign with the Miami Heat, many Cleveland fans were outraged. Some burned his numbered jersey. In their eyes, he had gone from hero to zero. Miami fans, on the other hand, celebrated LeBron's decision to play for the Heat. Opinions about sports stars and other celebrities may be wide ranging, but they are inconsequential as far as one's eternal destiny is concerned. Conversely, one's opinion of Jesus Christ has eternal consequences.

This study will help you explore opinions of Jesus that circulated when He ministered on earth and decide the correct one.

COMMENTARY

The paragraph break between John 5:15 and 16 seems to be a significant one. After the Sabbath healing of the paralyzed man, "the Jews [for the first time] persecuted [Jesus]" (5:16). They quickly moved to the point of wanting "to kill him" (5:18). Jesus did not back down. In fact, He went on the offensive, tying himself even closer to the Father (5:19–30). Jesus then defended His claims by alluding to a wide variety of witnesses who vouched for the authenticity of His identity and authority (5:31–47).

Chapter 6 records the feeding of a huge crowd. The Galilee townspeople conspired not to kill Jesus, but to make Him their king (6:1–15). But Jesus' difficult words about eating His flesh

and drinking His blood led many of His followers to forsake Him
(6:53–66).

John 7 opens with a glimpse of Jesus' brothers. They saw Him
as one seeking to become "a public figure" (v. 4). As Jesus arrived
in Jerusalem for the Jewish Feast of Tabernacles, others among the
anonymous crowds weighed in with their opinions: "He is a good
man" (v. 12); "He has deceived you" (v. 47). After hearing Jesus,
another group described Him as a learned person (v. 15; compare
v. 46). But for every positive evaluation, some other person or
group spoke a negative. Some bystanders slandered Jesus as they
addressed Him: "You are demon-possessed" (v. 20).

Who Is Jesus and Where Is He From? (John 7:25–32)

As John retold events in Jerusalem, he continued in the same
vein with which the chapter had opened. **"Isn't this the man they
are trying to kill?"** (v. 25). In other words, "Who is this man?"
Residents of Jerusalem had heard about a warrant out for Jesus'
arrest. If the man preaching publicly truly was Jesus, they could
not understand why the authorities did not throw Him in prison.

The common people spoke their confusion only among themselves. "No one would say anything publicly about [Jesus] for fear
of the Jews," those in authority (7:13). But in their homes and
shops, they began to wonder if the Jewish **authorities** had concluded (as some of the common people had, see 7:41) that Jesus
might be **the Christ** (v. 26). (**The Christ** was the long-awaited,
God-sent person who would bring freedom and power to Israel.)

The Jewish leaders struggled to recognize as messiah anyone
who did not fit in the box they had designed. They felt sure the
Christ would certainly recognize them as God's servants. He
would elevate them to the positions of national leadership they
knew they deserved. If this were true, Jesus could not be the
Christ. He spent more time with the common people than He did
with the big shots.

But even among the common people, who had far less to lose if an unexpected messiah revealed himself in Jerusalem, some doubted Jesus was the one. **"We know where this man is from; when the Christ comes, no one will know where he is from"** (v. 27). Today, we assume that all first-century Jews knew of Micah 5:2 as well as we do, that the Christ would come out of Bethlehem, out of David's line (see John 7:42). But even King Herod needed to consult his experts in order to gain that information (Matt. 2:3–5). At least some people in Jerusalem assumed (not altogether wrongly) that the first appearance of the Christ would involve mystery. Jesus' origins, however, were common knowledge. First-century detectives had already traced His family line back to Mary and Joseph of Nazareth.

WORDS FROM WESLEY

John 7:27

When Christ cometh, none knoweth whence he is—This Jewish tradition was true, with regard to His divine nature: in that respect none could *declare his generation*. But it was not true with regard to His human nature, for both His family and the place of His birth were plainly foretold. (ENNT)

Either through the rumor mill or divine insight, Jesus sensed what the people were saying. He spoke directly to their assumptions: **"You know me, and you know where I am from"** (John 7:28). Jesus reflected the people's perceptions of their knowledge, which, ironically, were both wrong. If they truly had known Jesus, they would have followed Him anywhere. If they had recognized Jesus' true origin, that He came from God (rather than Galilee), all their doubts would quickly have been erased. In their satisfaction with superficial facts, they missed the far deeper truths.

Who was this man, Jesus? In one sense, only the Father, an equally infinite Being who had interacted with the Son through an infinity of time, truly knew Him. The Father who perfectly knew Jesus **sent** Him to His own people (v. 29), those who should have recognized and worshiped Him. Unfortunately, God's people understood neither the Messiah concept nor that a man who stood before them fulfilled that very role (compare 1:1, 10–11).

Many people incorrectly saw Jesus as an imposter. They reasoned, "How can some local from Nazareth claim to have a closer relationship to God than we who live in God's chosen city?" One who falsely claimed to be sent from God deserved death. They attempted to **seize** Jesus, to give Him the punishment they felt He deserved, but found that impossible (7:30). At this point, the One who had sent Jesus protected Him from harm. Others, however, observing the same actions and hearing the same words, concluded that Jesus truly had come from God. They **put their faith in him** (v. 31). Note how John, throughout this chapter, carefully portrayed both sides of the debate. Countless people in Jesus' day, who knew that God existed and ruled, failed to recognize Him when He came.

Jesus was not the only one who heard the city rumors. Jesus heard and responded to those who rejected Him, but the Pharisees paid more attention to those who received Jesus as the Christ. Since civilians had failed to capture Jesus, the Jewish leaders sent in the troops. No ordinary person would be able to escape the clutches of the **temple guards** (v. 32). But, of course, as we know, Jesus was no ordinary person. The guards may have had the force to arrest Jesus, but Jesus had the verbal ability to, in effect, disarm them (7:46). Jesus spoke with a greater authority than the Pharisees ever could. The guards returned to their barracks without a prisoner. Instead, Jesus' offer of living water had caught them.

Who was this Jesus? The Father knew. Jesus knew. We know. The people of Jerusalem? They had not yet reached a consensus.

Jesus had given strong evidence, but His words and actions had elicited opposing responses.

Where Is Jesus Going? (John 7:33–36)

When the people disagreed over Jesus' identity despite all the hints He had given, Jesus, in effect, shifted the topic of conversation. He moved the debate from His commission to His destination: **"I am with you for only a short time, and then I go to the one who sent me. You will look for me, but you will not find me: and where I am, you cannot come"** (vv. 33–34). Again, we who have heard the end of the story clearly see at least part of Jesus' meaning. He was heading for a reunion with His Father, One whom the Pharisees had rejected in rejecting Jesus.

WORDS FROM WESLEY

John 7:34

Ye shall seek me — Whom ye now despise. These words are, as it were, the text which is commented upon in this and the following chapter. *Where I am* — Christ's so frequently saying while on earth, *where I am*, when He spake of His being in heaven, intimates His perpetual presence there in His divine nature: though His going thither was a future thing, with regard to His human nature. (ENNT)

In the riddle of Jesus' words, the Pharisees missed this meaning altogether. Another meaning, one more closely related to their attempt to arrest Jesus, also seemingly escaped them. They would not be able to capture Jesus that day, but He knew His time was coming. They would win one battle and send Jesus to His death, a destination they all wished to avoid.

The next paragraph lays out the Pharisees' puzzlement. Their best guess had Jesus going off to the Gentiles into territory they felt no desire to visit (v. 35).

Again, perhaps, we can see a veiled similarity to the content of the Synoptic Gospels. Matthew, Mark, and Luke all quoted Jesus teaching in parables, stories that left hearers to draw their own conclusions. Perhaps Jesus pictured His upcoming, mysterious, impossible-to-follow disappearance (vv. 33–34, 36) as a parable. His words offered no easy answers but, rather, further questions upon which honest seekers could reflect. (In this chapter, Jesus' close followers do not appear. One wonders how they would have interpreted His curious statements.)

Where Does Jesus Offer? (John 7:37–43)

Again, using images rather than concrete truth, Jesus spoke to the crowds. Note the **loud voice** with which He caught their attention (v. 37). **"If anyone is thirsty, let him come to me and drink. Whoever believes in me . . . streams of living water will flow from within him"** (vv. 37–38). Is there a reason Jesus chose this image for this particular day? He had earlier used the same image when sitting beside a well. His rationale for the water image that day is obvious still. What about this day?

John noted that Jesus spoke these words **on the last and greatest day of the Feast** (v. 37). Earlier in the chapter, John identified the festival as the "Feast of Tabernacles" (v. 2). During this eight-day-long celebration, God's people remembered the years that their ancestors had lived in the wilderness during the time between leaving Egypt and the conquest of Canaan. To get a feel for the ancient experience, Jews of subsequent generations moved out of their homes into shelters (or tabernacles) made of branches, remembering the camping lifestyle of their wandering ancestors. (See Lev. 23:39–43 for one description of this festival.) Over the centuries, the tradition arose that at the end of the tabernacles week, a priest carried water from a special local stream through the city into the temple and poured this water out on the altar, thus remembering God's miraculous provision of water for

His homeless ones waiting for the day when they could enter the Promised Land.

So on a day when the people were already thinking about water, Jesus proclaimed himself as the source of true **living water** (John 7:38). On this day, when the people might already have sung, "With joy [we] will draw water from the wells of salvation" (Isa. 12:3), Jesus opened those wells to all who heard and to all who still hear those words through Jesus' servant John.

WORDS FROM WESLEY

John 7:38

He that believeth—This answers to *let him come* to me. And whosoever doth come to Him by faith, his inmost soul shall be filled with *living water*, with abundance of peace, joy, and love, which shall likewise flow from him to others. *As the Scripture hath said*—Not expressly in any one particular place. But here is a general reference to all those Scriptures which speak of the *effusion of the Spirit* by the Messiah, under the similitude of *pouring out water*. (ENNT)

In case his own readers did not see the full picture, John helpfully filled in more of the colors (John 7:39). The water Jesus offered was not a substance to be manipulated. No, this water represented God's gift of himself, God come to live among (in Jesus) and within (in **the Spirit** [v. 39]) His people.

WORDS FROM WESLEY

John 7:38

It is of great importance to observe, and that more carefully than is commonly done, the wide difference there is between the Jewish and the Christian dispensation; and that ground of it which the same apostle assigns in the seventh chapter of his gospel. (Verses 38, &c.) After he had there related those words of our blessed Lord, "He that believeth on me, as the Scripture hath said, out of his belly shall flow rivers of living water," he immediately subjoins, "This spake he of the Spirit . . . *which they who should believe on him were afterwards to receive.* For the Holy Ghost was not yet given, because that Jesus was not yet glorified." Now, the apostle cannot mean here (as some have taught), that the miracle-working power of the Holy Ghost was not yet given. For this was given; our Lord had given it to all the apostles, when He first sent them forth to preach the gospel. He then gave them power over unclean spirits to cast them out; power to heal the sick; yea, to raise the dead. But the Holy Ghost was not yet given in His sanctifying graces, as He was after Jesus was glorified. It was then when "he ascended up on high, and led captivity captive," that He "received" those "gifts for men, yea, even for the rebellious, that the Lord God might dwell among them." And when the day of Pentecost was fully come, then first it was, that they who "waited for the promise of the Father" were made more than conquerors over sin by the Holy Ghost given unto them. (WJW, vol. 6, 10)

How did the people of Jerusalem respond to the gift Jesus offered? Once again, we see opposite responses.

Some excitedly reached their hands and hearts out to Jesus, seeing Him either as **the Prophet** or, yes, even, **the Christ** (vv. 40–41; Moses had predicted the coming of "a prophet" like himself, another illusive prediction of the coming of God's Son; see Deut. 18:15). Others voiced their skepticism: **The Christ** cannot **come from Galilee** (John 7:41). At least some of them remembered Micah's prophecy that the Messiah would arise out of **Bethlehem**, the home city of King **David** (v. 42).

not from Nazareth

John, in 7:43, summarized the entire chapter with these words: **The people were divided because of Jesus**. Their responses, however, ranged across the entire spectrum. Things have not changed. Many today willingly follow Jesus to the death. Others sneer at His claims and gifts. As it was then, the decision is left to each of us.

DISCUSSION

Opinions of Jesus vary greatly. Some people believe He was the Son of God. Some think He is just a man, perhaps a wise teacher or a martyr. Some consider Him a superhero. Some think He didn't exist. Reflect on who you say Jesus was (and is), and how this perception of Jesus has affected your life.

1. How do you explain the failure of Jesus' enemies to apprehend Jesus at this time?

2. How did Jesus predict His ascension?

3. Why did many in the crowd put their faith in Jesus? What do you think is currently the most persuasive factor in people's positive response to Jesus as Savior?

4. Compare Jesus' words in John 7:37–38 with Isaiah 12:3. What spiritual connection do you see between these passages?

5. How is it possible for streams of living water to flow from within a believer?

6. What would it take for your life to refresh others more fully?

7. Why were the people who heard Jesus divided in their opinion of Him?

PRAYER

Lord, we are thirsty. We want to drink deeply from the spring of living water. Thank You for giving Your Spirit that the spring may well up inside us. Help us to look to You alone to quench our thirst.

6

TIME IS LIMITED—BEWARE DISTRACTIONS

John 9:1–12, 28–41

Since the aim of evangelism is faith in Christ, we must
devote our attention to nothing less.

Recently, medical research has given ophthalmologists a new
tool and many patients new hope. A tiny telescope implanted in the
eye is helping some victims of macular degeneration see again. Can
you imagine what joy sight brings to a previously blind person?

Without using any technology, Jesus healed a man who had
been blind from birth, but not everyone was happy about it.
Some who opposed Jesus called Him a sinner, but the accusation
did not alter the fact that the miracle of sight had occurred.

Through this study, you will develop a stronger faith in Jesus,
and you will want to lead spiritually blind people to Jesus.

COMMENTARY

Jesus had been involved in a heated debate in the temple.
Sarcastically, the people had said He was not even fifty years
old, so how could He have known Abraham. He replied, "Before
Abraham was born, I am!" (John 8:58). They started to stone
Him, but Jesus hid himself and slipped out of the temple.

Sometime later the disciples joined Him, and as they walked,
Jesus saw a man blind from birth. This is the only reference to a
person with congenital blindness found in the New Testament. He
was a blind beggar and was apparently well-known even by the
disciples. He was a human being created for something better
than he was now experiencing. The man did not see Jesus, but
Jesus saw him, a man with a disability and great limitation.

The chapter begins and ends with a mission statement of Jesus—
"We must do the work of him who sent me. . . . I am the light of the
world. . . . For judgment I have come into this world, so that the
blind see and those who see will become blind" (9:4–5, 39).

Jesus is light to the blind man and also to the unbelieving in
this study. The light shines brighter to the believer, but it becomes
darkness to the unbelieving. John didn't use "believe" in the sense
of expecting to get something from God. Rather, he used it to
mean the affirmation of who a person is, such as the acceptance
of Jesus' message and the work He does. The revelation came both
to the blind man and to the doubting in stages.

The Man They Call Jesus (John 9:1–12)

Since Jesus was looking at the blind man, the disciples asked,
"Who sinned, this man or his parents?" (v. 2). The Jews at this
time believed that the sins of the fathers would be visited upon the
children even to the fourth generation (Ex. 20:5). They also
believed in prenatal sin—a child could sin in the womb—and in
the preexistence of the soul. Observe that Jesus did not really
answer their question, but said, **"So that the work of God might
be displayed in his life"** (John 9:3). God did not cause the blindness, but He was able to use the condition to reveal His mission: to
bring physical and spiritual wholeness to individuals. God would,
in this case, use His work of eliminating a disability, changing a
life made almost useless to one filled with potential. **We must do
the work of him who sent me** (v. 4). God had sent Jesus, and now
Jesus was sending the disciples—including them as part of the
workforce—to do the work of God. To **do the work** is a God-given
task that cannot be escaped. **Night is coming, when no one can
work** (v. 4). Note the contrasting words throughout the text—*work,
not work*; *day, night*; *darkness, light*; *blindness, sight*.

"While I am in the world, I am the light of the world"
(v. 5). Jesus becomes the means through which God is made

known. The light reveals God to people. Jesus used many ways to shed light on the hearts and minds of people: signs, wonders, miracles, storms, circumstances, seeds, birds, flowers. Jesus gave light to the blind eyes and soul of the man born blind. He comes from God, and "God is light" (1 John 1:5).

WORDS FROM WESLEY

John 9:4–5

4. *The night is coming*—Christ is the light. When the light is withdrawn, night comes, *When no man can work*—No man can do any thing towards working out his salvation after this life is ended. Yet Christ can work always. But He was not to work upon earth, only during the day, or season which was appointed for Him.

5. *I am the light of the world*—I teach men inwardly by my Spirit, and outwardly by my preaching, what is the will of God; and I show them, by my example, how they must do it. (ENNT)

The blind man was speechless until he returned home and his neighbors doubted his identity. He then replied, **"I am the man"** (John 9:9). He did not ask Jesus to heal him; Jesus came to him on His own initiative. Jesus did not talk with the man. He simply spat on the ground, made some mud, and put it on the man's eyes. The man allowed Jesus to do the work. He felt the touch of Jesus' fingers, and then he heard His voice when Jesus said, **"Go . . . wash in the Pool of Siloam"** (v. 7). The man went and washed and came home seeing. Jesus used a method—the usual, ordinary, and customary remedy of curing infected eyes—to channel His power of healing.

The healed man did not come back to Jesus; he went to his family and neighbors, those who knew him best. The man **came home seeing** (v. 7). His sight had not been restored; he had never had sight. He had a totally new creation of sight. Those who first realized the change in the man were his **neighbors and those**

who had formerly seen him begging (v. 8). They were so astonished that they questioned, **"Isn't this the same man who used
to sit and beg?"** (v. 8). Some said yes, but others claimed he
only looked like him. From sightlessness to sight made a great
change in the man's looks, facial expression, bearing, and manner
of conduct.

WORDS FROM WESLEY

John 9:7

Go, wash at the pool of Siloam—Perhaps our Lord intended to
make the miracle more taken notice of. For a crowd of people would
naturally gather round Him to observe the event of so a strange a
prescription, and it is exceeding probable, the guide who must have
led Him in traversing a great part of the city, would mention the
errand He was going upon, and so call all those who saw Him to a
greater attention. (ENNT)

However, the man **insisted, "I am the man"** (v. 9). They
found it difficult to identify him as the blind beggar. But the man
never doubted his identity. The world had changed. Things he
had never seen before were real and tangible. Voices now had
bodies and faces, but he knew who he was. The light began to
shine upon him, but the darkness began to settle down upon his
Jewish neighbors.

"How then were your eyes opened?" they demanded (v. 10).
He was not ashamed to say, **"The man they call Jesus made
some mud and put it on my eyes. He told me to go to Siloam
and wash."** Neither was he afraid to say, **"I went and washed,
and then I could see"** (v. 11).

The healed man must have known little about Jesus or His fame.
He merely knew Jesus' name and the miracle healing of his own
eyes. He had not seen Jesus make the mud plaster for his eyes.

He had only heard His voice and felt the touch of His hands on his eyelids. As far as he knew, Jesus was just a man. But the man born blind was not content to stay sightless if following Jesus' instructions would bring sight. He willingly accepted the command of Jesus and returned home with sight.

The Debate (John 9:28–34)

The blindness of the Jewish neighbors strengthened as they argued and debated whether Jesus was a sinner because He, in their minds, had broken the law of the Sabbath (vv. 13–34). No one could be from God who would do that, so they turned to the man again and asked, "What have you to say about him?" (v. 17). For him, the light was growing stronger and brighter: "He is a prophet" (v. 17). The revelation that came to him was stronger. His theological terms probably were imperfect, but he continued to tell it like it was: "I was blind but now I see!" (v. 25). He soon would be able to see more in the light that was shining upon him. **"We know that God does not listen to sinners. He listens to the godly man who does his will"** (v. 31).

WORDS FROM WESLEY

John 9:30

The man answered—Utterly illiterate as he was. And with what strength and clearness of reason! So had God opened the eyes of his understanding, as well as his bodily eyes. *Why, herein is a marvellous thing, that ye*—The teachers and guides of the people, should not know, that a man who has wrought a miracle, the like of which was never heard of before, must be from heaven, sent by God. (ENNT)

The darkness of the spiritual blindness was now settling thicker upon the Jewish neighbors and Pharisees. The simple man, born blind, was rebuking them for their unbelief and even quoting Scriptures to them. This reprimand was too much for them. They decided they would quiet him for good. So they threw him out of the synagogue. It is a strange truth; a person's truthful witness may cause a division between family, friends, and even church leaders.

The Man Is the Son of God (John 9:35–41)

The term **Son of Man** (v. 35) is translated "Son of God" in many of the old manuscripts. Jesus often referred to himself as the Son of Man, and He did not deny that He is the Son of God when Peter made his confession, "You are . . . the Son of the living God" (Matt. 16:16). The Father claims Him as His Son (Matt. 3:17). Jesus prayed to the Father, "Glorify your Son" (John 17:1). Son of God fits well here, for the healed man had just identified Jesus as from God when he said, "If this man were not from God, he could do nothing" (9:33).

This man had come from blindness to sight, but now he was without a church home. Jesus heard about the situation and sought to find the excommunicated man. **When he found him, he said, "Do you believe in the Son of Man?"** (v. 35). Instantly the man whom Jesus had healed said, **"Who is he, sir? . . . Tell me so that I may believe in him"** (v. 36). How eager the man was to know Him. Jesus didn't leave him dangling in confusion: **"You have now seen him; in fact, he is the one speaking with you"** (v. 37). The man makes full confession of his faith: **"Lord, I believe"** (v. 38). This is the climax—from what Jesus had done for him to a personal relationship with the Lord Jesus. Sight had been given to his blind eyes, which resulted in a revelation of who Jesus is.

He worshiped him (v. 38). Only God is worthy to be worshiped. Worship always follows belief. Worship is the complete act of surrender and submission of the self to the One worthy of honor, praise, and glory. Worship recognizes the holy God and the unworthy creature.

After realizing Jesus is the Son of God, the healed man called Him **Lord** (v. 38). He did not fully know all the theological ramifications of belief in Jesus as the Son of God, but he was convinced the One who said, **"You have now seen him; in fact, he is the one speaking with you"** (v. 37), was indeed God. He had imperfect faith and knowledge, but they were enough.

Jesus now turned His attention to the doubters, the unbelievers. How dark it had become for them. First, they challenged their own eyes: "This man can't be the blind beggar" (see v. 8). They questioned how his eyes were opened. They asked to be taken to the man who had given sight. Their religious teachings and heritage told them to seek out the educated teachers and have them take a look at the man. When they discovered Jesus had made mud and applied it to the man's eyes on the Sabbath day, they were astonished.

They fixed their minds on the thought that He could not be from God, that He was a sinner who broke the law. They even went so far as to say the man whom they had known for years as the blind beggar had not really been blind. They questioned his parents and suggested he was not their son who had been born blind. In their continued questioning of the man, they planted more seeds of darkness in their own minds. They rebuked the man and demanded he say that God had healed him, because in their minds, Jesus could not have healed. They insulted and degraded the man. It is dangerous to be disrespectful of another person. Their blindness increased as they became angry that a poor ignorant beggar could quote Scriptures they could not refute, so they put him out of the synagogue. How great their darkness had become.

"For judgment I have come into this world, so that the blind will see and those who see will become blind" (v. 39). The mission of Jesus coming into the world was not primarily that of answering the questions of why or of problem solving. He came to transform, banish blindness, and open eyes to see the Son of God. So in this text, Jesus showed not only God's power to correct and restore His creatures, but also God's judgment upon prejudiced and self-satisfied doubters who refuse to believe and accept Him, His message, and His works.

WORDS FROM WESLEY

John 9:39

For judgment am I come into the world—That is, the consequence of my coming will be, that by the just judgment of God, while the blind in body and soul receive their sight, they who boast they see, will be given up to still greater blindness than before. (ENNT)

"If you were blind, you would not be guilty of sin; but now that you claim you can see, your guilt remains" (v. 41). The Pharisees now claimed they knew more than Jesus. They had examined the facts, and they knew they were right and what He had said was wrong. Had they been blind—ignorant yet teachable—they could have accepted the truth. But they remained headstrong in their sinful doubting and continued to deny that Jesus is the Son of God. The light from God will never penetrate the darkness of one who refuses to accept and walk in the light He sheds upon the heart and mind.

Those who have knowledge of the Scriptures must put that knowledge into practice. "Do not merely listen to the word. . . . Do what it says" (James 1:22). These men were tried and found guilty because they knew and claimed to understand the Scriptures, yet they refused to believe in and recognize God's Son.

DISCUSSION

Just as Jesus lived with a sense of mission, He invites those who believe in Him to follow Him in the same mission—to proclaim the gospel wherever God leads us. *[handwritten: BELIEF - EVEN JESUS EARLEY]*
[handwritten: SINS OF THE FATHERS - 4TH GENERATION]

[left margin handwritten: WAGES OF SIN IS DEATH]
[left margin handwritten: SIN IS PARTING FROM GOD]

1. Why do some people assume physical infirmities and disabilities are caused by personal sin? *[handwritten: PARENTS/PRENATAL -WOMB]*

2. How does Jesus' statement in John 9:3 refute the notion that physical infirmity is always caused by personal sin? *[handwritten: WORK OF GOD MIGHT BE DISPLAYED - PHYSICAL & SPIRITUAL WHEREVER]*

3. How can a disabled or chronically ill Christian glorify God in his or her affliction? *[handwritten: HIS FAITH & BELIEF IN CHRIST - ALL FORGIVEN]*

[left margin handwritten: WARNING]

4. How do Jesus' words in verse 4 motivate you to seize every opportunity to serve God? *[handwritten: TO DO THE WORK OF GOD]*

5. Why did the blind beggar's neighbors struggle to identify him after Jesus had given him sight? *[handwritten: PHYSICAL CHANGE & Pg 56 TOP]*

6. What can you "see" as a Christian that you could not "see" before Jesus saved you? *[handwritten: KINDNESS, LOVE, GRACE, BELIEF]*
[handwritten: COMPASSION, AND GOD THE PERSON YOU COULD NOT LOVE HIM]

7. How did Jesus' enemies respond to the healing of the blind man? *[handwritten: ACCUSED OF SINNING ON SABBATH. DISRESPECTED HIM, REFUSED TO ACCEPT]*

8. How did the healed man show that Jesus had also made his soul whole? *[handwritten: ACCEPTED COMMAND OF JESUS RETURNED HOME WITH SIGHT]*
[handwritten: He IS THE PROPHET - FROM GOD " I BELIEVE " WORSHIPPED HIM]

[left margin handwritten: LORD I BELIEVE]

PRAYER

Lord, open our eyes so we see You. Help us to not be blinded by our pride, convinced that we are seeing everything perfectly.

[handwritten notes at bottom: PHILIPPIANS 4:4, 3; PAUL]
[handwritten: PHARISEES NOT UNGODLY WENT TOO FAR BEYOND LAW DOGMAS]
[handwritten: (14)]
[handwritten: GREAT GRANDSON, DALE ANYA, RED, KOBUS -SCOOTY, DICK - JOSIAH-SHISHA, DELGADO]

7

THE ONLY WAY TO GOD

John 10:1–18

———————————

Although it sounds narrow to modern culture,
Jesus is the only way to God.

Wyoming sheep ranchers have a problem. The promise of better pay in the oil and gas fields has been luring hired sheepherders away from their sheep. Perhaps working in the oil and gas fields is somehow more attractive than tending sheep. A shepherd must get up around 4:00 a.m. with the sheep and stay with them until they bed down after sunset, all for roughly eight hundred dollars a month plus room and board.

This study focuses on Jesus, the Good Shepherd, who guards His sheep, knows each of them by name, and leads them by the sound of His voice. He even gave His life for His sheep.

COMMENTARY

This study focuses on the Good Shepherd, Jesus, who is also the only way to God. In the pervious study, which was taken from chapter 9, John told the story of Jesus' healing the man who had been born blind. After he was healed, the leaders of the Jews excommunicated him from the synagogue because he professed belief in Jesus. Chapter 9 closed with Jesus noting ironically that "the blind will see and those who see will become blind" (John 9:39).

Notes in the *NIV Study Bible* suggest that John 10 is an allegory based on the story of the blind man who had been healed. The Good Shepherd (Jesus) shows the true way for the sheep to follow; thieves and robbers (the Jewish leaders) pose as shepherds only to prey on the sheep. The Pharisees and the teachers of the law are false shepherds who continually challenge the words and works of Jesus. This theme had been developed in the Old Testament, where God is pictured as David's Shepherd (Ps. 23) and the "Shepherd of Israel" (Ps. 80:1–2; Isa. 40:10–11; Ezek. 34). Likewise, prophets who misled or took advantage of the people were pictured as false shepherds (Isa. 56:9–12; Ezek. 34:2–10).

Numerous contrasts between the Good Shepherd and the false shepherds are given throughout this passage. The teaching about Jesus, the Good Shepherd, is clear. In like manner, the teaching about the Jewish leaders ("the Jews") is clear: they maliciously threw out the new believer whom Jesus had healed of blindness. He now could see, but the offending Jewish leaders were blind.

Following the discourse on the Good Shepherd is another description of antagonism and controversy between Jesus and the Jewish leaders. He again rebukes their unbelief, carrying on with the theme of the Shepherd and His sheep. "You do not believe because you are not my sheep. My sheep listen to my voice; I know them, and they follow me" (10:26–27).

The Good Shepherd and His Relation to His Flock (John 10:1–6)

A good shepherd can be recognized by several characteristics. First, he enters the sheepfold through the gate. The sheepfold was designed to keep the sheep together and protect them from wild animals or other dangers. It had only one entrance, and that entrance would have been guarded overnight by a watchman. When morning came, the shepherd would come for his flock to take them out to pasture. Thieves and robbers only came to the sheepfold to do harm, "to steal and kill and destroy" (John 10:10). They did not come through the gate, because they feared the watchman who guarded it.

Second, the watchman also recognizes a good shepherd and allows him to enter when he comes to the gate. Other intruders are turned away by the watchman.

Third, the sheep recognize the voice of the shepherd. Several flocks might be mingled together in the safety of the sheepfold, but the sheep recognize the voice of their shepherd and follow him out to pasture. The voice of the shepherd is all that is needed to sort individual sheep into their respective flocks.

WORDS FROM WESLEY

John 10:3

And the sheep hear his voice—The circumstances that follow, exactly agree with the customs of the ancient eastern shepherds. They *called their sheep by name, went before them*, and the sheep *followed* them. So real Christians hear, listen to, understand, and obey the voice of the shepherd whom Christ hath sent. And he counteth them *his own*, dearer than any friend or brother: *calleth*, advises, directs each *by name*, and *leadeth them out*, in the paths of righteousness, beside the waters of comfort. (ENNT)

Fourth, a good shepherd has spent much time with his flock, and he knows and calls each of the sheep by name. To the outsider, sheep within a flock are generally indistinguishable, but to the shepherd, each sheep is an individual subject to his tender care. On the other hand, the sheep will often run from a stranger, and the intruder would have great trouble, if not an impossible task, trying to sort and organize them into a flock, since the sheep **do not recognize a stranger's voice** (v. 5). But **when he has brought out all his own,** the shepherd **goes on ahead of them, and his sheep follow him because they know his voice** (v. 4).

Many analogies to the thieves and robbers might be made. The immediate comparison was clear: the Jewish leaders were playing that role. It seems accurate to portray many cults as thieves also, for they often have presented the way to God as depending on some other revelation or device besides Christ and His cross. Often works have figured prominently as the way to God.

WORDS FROM WESLEY

John 10:4

He goeth before them—In all the ways of God, teaching them in every point, by example as well as by precept; *and the sheep follow him*—They tread in his steps: *for they know his voice*—Having the witness in themselves that his words are *the wisdom and the power of God*. Reader, art thou a shepherd of souls? Then answer to God. Is it thus with thee and thy flock? (ENNT)

The crowds **did not understand what** Jesus **was telling them** (v. 6). Perhaps it was because they did not want to understand. To clarify His meaning, Jesus continued His teaching about the good shepherd and the impostors.

The Gate for the Sheep (John 10:7–10)

"I tell you the truth, I am the gate for the sheep" (v. 7). Jesus shifted the analogy somewhat with this statement. It is one "I am" descriptions of Jesus that is in the gospel (John 8:12; 9:5; 10:7, 9, 11, 14; 11:25; 14:6 15:1, 5). Each saying may be thought of in light of God's self-description to Moses in Exodus 3:14: "I AM WHO I AM." They are a strong affirmation of the deity of Jesus Christ, the God-Man.

Here Jesus described himself as the very entrance to God and salvation. He is the way to God. Though it is not stated explicitly that He is the only way to God, it seems implicitly true, since all others are described as **thieves and robbers** (John 10:8). Jesus does make it explicit in John 14:6: "I am the way and the truth and the life. No one comes to the Father except through me."

Some commentators believe this statement, **"I am the gate for the sheep"** (10:7), reflects the fact that the shepherd would lie in the gate to guard the sheep whenever no watchman was available. With his body, the shepherd prevented the sheep from straying and prevented intruders from entering through the gate. However, it seems that Jesus went beyond that analogy by claiming not only to be the shepherd who leads the sheep to God and salvation, but also to be the actual entrance through which they must come to be saved. **"I am the gate; whoever enters through me will be saved. He will come in and go out, and find pasture"** (v. 9). Through the Good Shepherd, the sheep are saved, and they also find sustenance as they go in and out and find pasture. Through His tender care, the Good Shepherd supplies all their needs.

In contrast, **"The thief comes only to steal and kill and destroy; I have come that they may have life, and have it to the full"** (v. 10). Though this is true, the sad fact remains that many choose to affiliate with thieves, who kill and destroy, rather than to trust in the Good Shepherd, who gives eternal life. They foolishly choose death and destruction rather than life. They turn from the light and choose the darkness because their deeds are evil (3:19). Nevertheless, Jesus tried to warn and persuade those who heard Him (and those of us who read this record) to avoid false shepherds like the Jewish leaders of His day. **The sheep did not listen to them** (10:8). Still today, the sheep will not listen to them but follow the Good Shepherd.

The Good Shepherd's Ultimate Act (John 10:11–13)

The analogy is not yet complete. Jesus gives another "I am" statement: **"I am the good shepherd"** (vv. 11, 14). Furthermore, as the Good Shepherd, He lays down his life for the sheep (v. 11). Here we have another clear allusion to His death that was coming soon. A good shepherd does not give first consideration to his own safety, but to the safety of his sheep. Jesus prayed, "Father, if you are willing, take this cup from me; yet not my will, but yours be done" (Luke 22:42). It was not the Father's will to take the cup, and Jesus proceeded through humiliation and cruel affliction to the cross and death. Jesus made this ultimate sacrifice for His sheep so they can now enter through him and be saved (John 10:9).

The hired hand works only for what he can get out of the job, for personal benefit. Thus, when he sees the wolf coming, he takes care of himself and abandons the sheep. **Then the wolf attacks the flock and scatters it. The man runs away because he is a hired hand and cares nothing for the sheep** (vv. 12–13). Only the good shepherd loves the sheep and is willing to forget his own safety in order to protect them. The contrast between Jesus, the Good Shepherd, and the antagonistic Jewish leaders is obvious. They had thrown the new believer whom Jesus had healed of blindness out of the synagogue. They repeatedly attacked Jesus as a false prophet, a false shepherd. But Jesus did not speak empty words; His words were soon fulfilled on a Roman cross in Jerusalem. The Good Shepherd did lay down His life for the sheep in order to save them.

WORDS FROM WESLEY
John 10:12

But the hireling—It is not the bare *receiving* hire, which denominates a man an hireling: (for *the labourer is worthy of his hire*; Jesus Christ himself being the judge: yea, and the *Lord hath ordained, that they who preach the Gospel, should live of the Gospel*) . . . He is an hireling, who would not work, were it not for the hire; to whom this is the great (if not only) motive of working. O God! If a man who works only *for hire*, is such a wretch, a mere *thief and a robber*, what is he who continually takes the hire, and yet does not work at all? (ENNT)

The Purpose of the Father (John 10:14–18)

In this paragraph, John quoted Jesus as He taught profound theological concepts concerning the purpose of God. There is mutual knowledge between the Good Shepherd and the sheep just as there is mutual knowledge between the Son and the Father. The Father's wonderful plan of salvation laid before the foundation of the world (Eph. 4:1–10) is known by Jesus and is being worked out in His life and death.

Jesus then stated that He would **lay down** His **life for the sheep** (John 10:15). The reaction to His statement was divided. Some thought Him demon-possessed or mad (vv. 19–20), but others recognized His words were not from one demon-possessed. Besides, they could hardly ignore the fact that He had cured one who was born blind (v. 21).

Jesus then alluded to the fact that He had other sheep besides those in the fold. Evidently **this sheep pen** (v. 16) is a reference to the Jewish people. **"I must bring them also. They too will listen to my voice, and there shall be one flock and one shepherd"** (v. 16). This is one of Jesus' clearest statements about the fact that Gentiles would also believe and be saved. The division between Jew and Gentile would be removed to form one flock.

The profound fact is that God's loving purpose for sending His Son was to allow Him to die for the sheep. **"The reason my Father loves me is that I lay down my life—only to take it up again"** (v. 17). The Father's love for the Son was not dependent on the Son's sacrifice of His own life, but it was inextricably connected to His purpose of redeeming humankind. Wonderfully, death was not the end; the Son would take up His life again, and that through His own power.

Jesus' death was part of the Father's plan, but it was also entirely voluntary. **"No one takes it from me, but I lay it down of my own accord. I have authority to lay it down and authority to take it up again. This command I received from my Father"** (v. 18). These profound words summarize the plan of salvation. The Father commanded the Son to lay down His life for the sheep. The Son was not forced to lay down His life, but He voluntarily did so. The whole plan was bathed in divine love between Father and Son, and between the Good Shepherd and the sheep. Wonder of wonders, death did not end the work of the Good Shepherd, for He would return to life again, demonstrating His eternal power over death and sin.

WORDS FROM WESLEY

John 10:18

I lay it down of myself—By my own free act and deed. *I have power to lay it down and I have power to take it again*—I have an original power and right of myself, both to lay it down as a ransom, and to take it again, after full satisfaction is made, for the sins of the whole world. *This commission have I received of my Father*—Which I readily execute. . . . Our Lord's receiving this commission as mediator, is not to be considered as the ground of His power to lay down and resume His life. For this He had in himself, as having an original right to dispose thereof, antecedent to the Father's commission. But this commission was the reason why He thus used His power in laying down His life. He did it in obedience to His Father. (ENNT)

This is a wonderful description of God's love and the infinite price He paid to redeem His sheep. The mystery of God's ways and purpose surpasses our ability to comprehend it all. Theologians have done their best to explain the atonement with limited success, and we are grateful for their insights. The simple truth is easy to understand: We enter the sheepfold through the gate, Jesus the Good Shepherd, who gave His life for the sheep and then took His life back again. Then, though we may not understand very much in the way of profound theology, we know we are saved because we trust the Good Shepherd and what He has done. Humbly, we give thanks!

DISCUSSION

Many people in modern culture are suspicious of those who
claim to know ultimate truth; but Scripture teaches that the truth
is a person—Jesus the Lord. *PROTECTION - SHEEP IS / DANGER OUT*

1. Why did a sheep pen have only one entrance?

2. How did the shepherd in Bible times lead his sheep to
pasture? *BY HIS VOICE / BY NAME / TRUST*

3. How can a believer distinguish the voice of the Good
Shepherd from that of a false shepherd? *LISTENS TO HIS VOICE AND FOLLOW*

4. How has a false shepherd tried to lead you astray? Were
you able to resist that seduction? How? If not, ask the Good
Shepherd to help you in the future. *LORDS PRAYER*

5. Based on John 10:3, how do you know the Good Shepherd
wants a personal relationship with you? *KNOWS MY NAME HE HAS CALLED OUT AND I HAVE FOLLOWED*

6. According to verse 10, why did Jesus come into the world?

7. How do you know from John 10:11–18 that Jesus' death
on the cross was not an accident? *IT WAS PLANNED BY GOD lays his life down for his sheep*

8. Why is verse 16 especially meaningful to you? *ALL PEOPLE NOT JUST THE JEWS + GENTILES*

PRAYER

Thank You, Jesus, for laying down Your life for our sakes!
Thank You for caring for us as a Good Shepherd and for knowing
us by name. Help us hear Your voice and follow You wherever
You may lead.

JESUS GIVES LIFE

John 11:1–4, 17–27, 38–44

A study of the miracle is a glimpse into the power of God
to change the humanly impossible.

Mortuaries seldom, if ever, go out of business. Even in tough economic times, people need a mortician, because loved ones die.

The death of a loved one is traumatic, but Jesus cares. He wept at the tomb of Lazarus. But Jesus also is the Resurrection and the Life. All who believe in Him go to be with Him when they die. Furthermore, Christians anticipate a glad day of reunion; no one is ever lost if we know that person is in heaven.

This study will help you see Jesus as the One who conquered death and who gives life to all who believe in Him.

COMMENTARY

Jesus used the word *sleep* for death. Sleep does not cause one to cease to be, but merely makes the person unconscious and unaware of surroundings and happenings. When awakened, the person is restored to awareness. On the physical level, death is the separation of spirit and body. That was what Jesus was thinking when He said Lazarus was "asleep." His spirit was separated from his body, but he did not cease to be—he was still Lazarus.

On the spiritual level, death is separation of the soul from God. Jesus came to die on the cross so that no one should be eternally separated from God. The disciples did not want to return to Judea. They were fearful not only for Jesus, but also for themselves. But Jesus said to them, "My work is not finished." The "twelve hours of daylight" (John 11:9) are hours in which anyone can work. When night comes, it is dark and no one can see to work. He did not want the disciples to be fearful, because He had not reached the end of His working day. He could not stop doing God's will during the twelfth hour because He was afraid to die. He was on God's timetable, and He would do nothing to disrupt that schedule. When darkness prevailed, His enemies would become the stumbling blocks that brought His work to an end.

The disciples knew that humankind could struggle, fight, and sometimes overcome diseases; but they thought there was no help adequate to overcome death. Jesus could, for their sakes, prove His power over death, reveal His purpose in coming to earth, and at the same time strengthen their belief in Him as the Messiah. On two other occasions, He had restored life to a person who had just died—Jairus's daughter and the son of the widow at Nain. But Lazarus had been dead for four days! "For your sake I am glad I was not there" (John 11:15). If Jesus had been present, Lazarus would not have died, and the disciples would not have seen the sign of His messiahship. They would need this sign for assurance, encouragement, and strength as they watched Him walk the Calvary road. He knew this final miracle would lead to the cross and His death, and they would need to know with certainty who He was.

Love for Friends Would Lead to His Own Death (John 11:1–4)

Jesus left Jerusalem and went to Perea to escape those who sought to kill Him. It was here that He received the message: **"Lord, the one you love is sick"** (v. 3). Martha, the oldest; Lazarus, the youngest; and Mary, the one who would pour expensive perfume on Jesus' feet, were His friends. The message did not request Him to come. It was assumed that the Friend who loved them would come if He knew the need.

WORDS FROM WESLEY

John 11:1

One Lazarus—It is probable, Lazarus was younger than his sisters. Bethany is named, the town of Mary and Martha, and Lazarus is mentioned after them, ver. 5. Ecclesiastical history informs us, that Lazarus was now thirty years old, and that he lived thirty years after Christ's ascension. (ENNT)

"This sickness will not end in death" (v. 4). Jesus was aware this illness would result in an earthly death. He also knew He could have prevented this death. **"No, it is for God's glory so that God's Son may be glorified through it"** (v. 4). The sickness would be the means of revealing God's glory, and the Son would be glorified because Lazarus's death would ultimately bring about Jesus' death (v. 53). John used this expression **glorified** to mean the coming cross, Jesus' death, and His return to glory (7:39; 12:16, 23–24; 13:31–32). He also used it in conjunction with the Father (5:23; 8:54–58; 10:30, 38). Look at 11:45–57 and see that the resurrection of Lazarus did result in many believing in Jesus, while others began to plot how they would kill Him.

The sickness would not have death as a final result. Jesus saw death and the resurrection as facts, true events that would take place. Life would be the end, not death. Jesus knew that helping His friend would lead to His own death, but He was determined to do the will of the Father.

Earthly Death and Resurrection Life (John 11:17–27)

Jesus remained in Perea for two more days, then He and the disciples returned to Judea. Jesus said, "Let us go back to Judea" (v. 7), the land of hostility, not to Bethany, the place of love and friendship. When they arrived near the village, **Jesus found that**

Lazarus had already been in the tomb for four days (v. 17).
This indicates that Lazarus had died and was buried the day Jesus
received the message. Burial was on the same day of death
because of the hot climate. **Many Jews had come to Martha
and Mary to comfort them** (v. 19). There was customarily four
days of weeping with the survivors. **When Martha heard that
Jesus was coming, she went out to meet him** (v. 20). Martha was
the woman of action (Luke 10:38–42). She was never idle and
always took the lead. Martha spoke from her heart. **"Lord . . . if
you had been here"** (John 11:21). She showed confidence in her
friend, even if He was too late to help her brother. **"But I know
that even now God will give you whatever you ask"** (v. 22).
She had expressed her deep regret, but she believed God would
answer Jesus' prayers. She did not know what He would ask
from the Father, but she was confident Jesus was truly interested
in her, so He would ask for whatever He felt would be best for
her.

Jesus knew something more than Martha. He knew the present; Lazarus was physically dead. But Jesus also knew the near
and distant future; He had a complete view of life. **"Your
brother will rise again"** (v. 23). That was poor consolation for
her, because she knew only the present. Her answer, **"I know he
will rise again in the resurrection at the last day"** (v. 24),
reveals that limited knowledge. She had accepted this as a statement of creed, but for the present time, there was no hope; it was
too late. Her idea of resurrection was not an accepted thought
by everyone at that time.

Jesus said to her (v. 25). The message was for her today. She
was to turn from her grief to Him. **"I am the resurrection"**
(v. 25). The reality is, **I am**. He did not need to pray to the Father.
There was no need to think in terms of the future general resurrection. **"I am the resurrection,"** a fact identified with His person
and the resurrection. Jesus is life. This was His last opportunity to

demonstrate this message before the unbelieving Jews who planned to kill Him. Jesus is essential and eternal life that begins when a person believes in Him, His message, and His mission on earth (John 3:16). **"He who believes in me will live, even though he dies"** (11:25). Jesus is life, and this life is not affected by earthly death. This life cannot be physical, bodily life, for all humankind—believers and unbelievers alike—experience physical death. This is the spiritual life for those who were dead in trespasses and sin and who crossed over from death to life in Christ (5:24–27). This life is eternal in that it has no end and is not interrupted by physical death.

What a great, eternal truth Jesus gave to a woman in sorrow: **"I am the resurrection and the life"** (11:25)! He is life—resurrection life—to all who believe in Him. Notice Jesus didn't say the one who believes will live again or be restored to life. That person will **live** and **never die** (vv. 25–26).

"Do you believe this?" (v. 26). What is **this**? Belief in (1) the "I am," the person and character of Jesus; (2) His work and relationship to life—"the resurrection and the life"; (3) "in me"—the way the gift of life is given; and (4) "whoever lives and believes will never die"—the Giver gives life to physically dying persons. Jesus is divine love in all its redemptive activity for all humankind. But only those who believe this will receive life eternal.

In Martha's answer, **"Yes, Lord, . . . I believe that you are the Christ, the Son of God, who was to come into the world"** (v. 27), she used the three titles for the Messiah: **the Christ**, **Son of God**, and One sent into the world. She recited it as a creed and as if it had not yet captured and motivated her. She believed He had the power to be the Messiah, but she wasn't really aware how this affected her. Her brother was dead and she vaguely hoped that in some way her household could be restored to normal.

Physical Resurrection (John 11:38–44)

Jesus had been "deeply moved in spirit and troubled" (v. 33). He wept with utmost grief, for both He and His friends were experiencing the loss of one they loved. They led Him to the tomb, and again He was **deeply moved** (v. 38).

Jesus instructed them, **"Take away the stone"** (v. 39). Immediately, Martha objected. She could see only the lifeless, decaying corpse wrapped in grave clothes. That is what everyone believed they would see. Decay would have set in after four days and would have resulted in unbearable odors. Her brother had died in dignity. She did not want the disfigurement of the corruption and decay of the fleshly body to be exposed to the curious eyes of others. Jesus could see the decay of an earthly body, but He saw more—the same man, Lazarus, a living resurrected person. **"Did I not tell you that if you believed, you would see the glory of God?"** (v. 40).

The stone was removed so the crowd would be able to see Lazarus come from within the tomb. Jesus **looked up** (v. 41) and prayed to the Father. He was conscious of His divine power and of the cooperation of the Father-and-Son relationship that did the work of God. They were constantly one in plan, purpose, and mission. He was aware of this oneness. The prayer was not to persuade God to honor Jesus by using God's power to perform the miracle of restored life. This public prayer was said for the unbelieving Jews to hear. His request was for the scoffing unbelievers to witness one more time that He is the One sent from God. The tomb was opened; the crowd was waiting. There was great suspense. Everything depended on the outcome. Jesus was who He said He was, or He was an impostor. This miracle would prove His claim was either true or false—**"that they may believe that you sent me"** (v. 42).

> ## WORDS FROM WESLEY
> *John 11:41*
>
> *Jesus lifted up his eyes*—Not as if He applied to His Father for assistance. There is not the least show of this. He wrought the miracle with an air of absolute sovereignty, as the Lord of life and death. But it was as if He had said, I thank thee, that by the disposal of thy providence, thou hast granted my desire, in this remarkable opportunity, of exerting my power, and showing forth thy praise. (ENNT)

Jesus called in a loud voice (v. 43). The **loud voice** was neither necessary for the miracle to take place, nor to awaken Lazarus. It was for the benefit of the crowd. **"Lazarus, come out!"** (v. 43). Jesus singled out Lazarus so the crowd would know who was coming out and also lest all the other dead would come forth also (see John 5:25). Lazarus was absent from his body; but wherever he was, he heard, recognized, and obeyed the voice of Jesus. Jesus and Lazarus had a bond that was not broken by death.

Jesus was the one person in the crowd who was not surprised or awestruck. **The dead man came out, his hands and feet wrapped with strips of linen, and a cloth around his face** (11:44). How Lazarus must have struggled to sit, stand, and walk out of that cave bound like this! **"Take off the grave clothes"** (v. 44). Those who removed the grave clothes touched a live Lazarus, the man who had been dead for four days. Perhaps Jesus said, **"Let him go"** (v. 44), because Lazarus needed to get away from the excitement and curiosity of the crowd as well as to be free to move.

WORDS FROM WESLEY

John 11:47

What do we? — What? Believe. Yea, but death yields to the power of Christ sooner than infidelity. (ENNT)

This miracle lets us see Jesus as He relates to us. He reveals His sorrow, love, and grief, as well as the power of friendship. He indeed was made flesh (John 1:14).

This final miracle did cause some to believe in Him. Others rushed in unbelief to tell the Pharisees, who hastened their plot to kill Him. Truly, the Son moved on rapidly to the way of the cross and death. The plan of redemption would soon be completed.

DISCUSSION

Death and dying are unpleasant subjects, but everyone must die eventually. However, Jesus holds the power over death. Review the verses of this study and reflect on which one you find most comforting as you think about death. *BELIEVER* *ONE WHO SERVES*

1. Why did Jesus stay two days where He was after hearing that Lazarus was sick? *SEE HIS MESSIASHIP* *BELIEVING* *STAYED* *SMITH* *ACTION GATHER*

2. What personality differences do you see in Mary and Martha?

3. In what sense does a believer in Jesus never die? *BELIEF IN JESUS PHYSICAL/ETERNAL*

BELIEVE HE WAS CHRIST/SON OF GOD 4. Read John 11:27. How did Martha show strong faith in Jesus?

NON BELIEVER 5. Why do you think Jesus wept at Lazarus's tomb? *HIS FRIEND COULD HAVE PREVENTED DEATH*

BELIEVE 6. According to verse 42, what was the primary purpose of the miracle of Jesus' raising Lazarus from the dead?

7. Why do you think Jesus called Lazarus by name to leave the tomb? *FOR BENEFIT OF THOSE WATCHING*

8. Read Romans 6:4. How has Jesus freed you from sin? What is the proof that He has raised you from bondage to sin? *(JESUS) BURIED WITH HIM THROUGH BAPTISM.*

PRAYER

Thank You, Jesus, for showing Your power over death by raising Lazarus from the grave. Help us to have the right perspective on our own suffering and to seek Your glory above all else.

WEPT FOR UNBELIEVERS HIS OWN DEATH

WE ARE SAVED BY JESUS WITHOUT SIN.

9

SERVING AS JESUS SERVED

John 13:1–17

———————

Godly leaders lead by serving.

A job interviewer must grow tired of hearing self-serving applicants boast about their skills and accomplishments. However, occasionally an applicant seems both highly skilled and humble. That person makes an interviewer's day.

Jesus exemplified humble service by washing His disciples' feet. This study will challenge you to serve others in Jesus' name.

COMMENTARY

The previous study focused on the Lazarus story (John 11). Here, we consider the opening verses of John 13. Before reviewing Jesus' interaction with His disciples in the upper room, let's briefly review chapter 12.

Chapter 12 records four distinct vignettes. These four balance each other in an astounding way. The chapter opens with Mary of Bethany pouring her devotion upon the Jesus she loved. She risked her reputation in demonstrating her love lavishly (12:1–3). The chapter closes with two opposite pictures. The first shows people who did not believe, whose blindness prevented them from seeing the light (12:39–40). A second picture, almost as sad, shows people who did believe, but hid their true thoughts and feelings under a basket (see Matt. 5:15). "They would not confess their faith for fear they would be put out of the synagogue; for they loved praise from men more than praise from God" (John 12:42–43).

The two central segments of John 12 contrast each other with equal strength. John 12:12–19 details how Jerusalem crowds "hosannaed" Jesus into the national capital—Jesus' greatest moment of acclamation and celebration. Then, John 12:20 pictures a few Gentiles approaching Jesus, not knowing much, but eager for more. Jesus seemingly recognized this as a signal of the coming trial. He moved into a soliloquy of desolation: "Now my heart is troubled, and what shall I say? 'Father, save me from this hour'? No, it was for this very reason I came to this hour. Father, glorify your name!" (12:27–28). With resolve, Jesus turned His mind from the adoration He had received throughout His days to the cross the Father erected before His Son.

Nearing the end of His public ministry, Jesus offered the light one last time before the darkness fell. Having given himself to the crowds over three years, Jesus moved away from them, not out of self-preservation, but so He might give himself to them in the most significant way: His death. "When he had finished speaking, Jesus left and hid himself from them" (12:36). Those verses set the context for the next five chapters in which Jesus interacts first with His disciples and then alone with His Father.

John Set the Stage (John 13:1)

It was just before the Passover Feast (v. 1). So often we hope that this story will turn out differently, that all God's people will realize they are kin, that together they will bow down before God in the flesh. It never happens. While we know we can read again of the resurrection, the fact that the story ends well does not relieve all the pain of the great battle we know is coming.

John's gospel has laid all the background—three years, two previous Passovers, many times when John declared that Jesus' enemies could do nothing against Him, that His time had not yet come. But in John 12, the tune changed. Jesus' hour had come (12:23). Then when John so plaintively pointed out that Passover time had come again, that once again the people would shed blood as a sign of God's protection, he began to signal the identity of that year's Lamb.

Jesus knew that the time had come for him to leave this world and go to the Father (13:1). John began his narrative with Jesus' arrival from the Father: "The Word [who had been] with God [and yet] was God . . . became flesh and made his dwelling among us" (1:1, 14). With 13:1, the ferry is about to reverse direction and take its divine passenger back home.

Having loved his own who were in the world (13:1). With these words, John summarized his first twelve chapters, the first three years of Jesus' ministry—to His disciples, His people, His opponents. **He now showed them the full extent of his love** (v. 1). As the first half of this verse looked back, the second half looks forward. Both halves can be read on several levels, revealing several concentric circles of love. At what point did Jesus show the full extent of His love? In the foot washing that followed immediately? In His words of hope and concern for the disciples' well-being hours before His own tribulation? In the struggle in the garden? On the cross? In His death? This multiple-choice question calls for "all of the above." Throughout the events recorded in John 13–19, in a historically unprecedented and never-to-be-matched manner, Jesus demonstrated the full extent of His love.

Jesus Washed the Disciples' Feet (John 13:2–5)

After this chapter's breathtaking overture, John's next words sound a much quieter note: **The evening meal was being served** (v. 2). In the other three gospels, the last meal Jesus ate with His inner circle was the Passover meal. The other three evangelists clearly identified the historic Passover with the new Passover meal, Jesus forever transforming the meaning of bread and wine.

In John's account, the last meal itself held no special significance. The Passover was to be celebrated the next day. In this plan, Jews around the city, the Empire, were sacrificing their four-legged lambs at or near the moment when God was offering His own Lamb for the world.

Do we need to harmonize these two accounts? That might be neat and clean, but in our tidiness, we might be eliminating something of value from one of the narratives. Perhaps there is something to learn from both tellings of these history-changing twenty-four hours. Their eternal truth and meaning far overshadow any matter of mere chronology.

During something as mundane as an evening meal, the spirit world was quaking. **The devil had already prompted Judas Iscariot, son of Simon, to betray Jesus** (v. 2). The deal had already been struck (see Mark 14:10–11). John subsequently noted that, a few minutes later, Satan himself "entered into" Judas (13:27). Jesus knew what was coming. Judas knew he would soon play his role. Satan felt sure he had won.

A crucial word begins verse 4: **so**. How can this be? John 13:3 returns to the grandeur of the great plan. **Jesus knew** about His divine **power** and His divinely ordained human pain. Despite all power being given to Jesus (see Matt. 28:18)—the power through which Jesus could choose to save the world or himself— He became a servant. Despite the approaching hour during which Jesus would bear the pain of all past, present, and future human population, Jesus moved into a simple task that His disciples— Judas included—would never forget.

Not only despite the power and the pain, but somehow because of all Jesus was and would do, He **wrapped a towel around his waist . . . poured water into a basin and began to wash his disciples' feet** (John 13:4–5). This task was usually left to the lowest servant. The ancients maneuvered city streets and country lanes on foot, wearing leather soles with only a few strings holding them in place. Their feet ended up covered with dust or mud.

WORDS FROM WESLEY

John 13:5

Jesu, by highest heavens adored,
The church's glorious Head;
With humble joy I call Thee, Lord,
And in Thy footsteps tread.
Emptied of all Thy greatness here
While in the body seen,
Thou wouldst the least of all appear,
And minister to men.
A servant to Thy servants Thou
In Thy debased estate,
How meekly did Thy goodness bow
To wash Thy followers' feet!
And shall a worm refuse to stoop,
His fellow-worms disdain?
I give my vain distinctions up,
Since God did wait on man.
At charity's almighty call
I lay my greatness by,
The least of saints, I wait on all,
The chief of sinners I.
Happy, if I their grief may cheer,
And mitigate their pain,
And wait upon the servants here,
Till with the Lord I reign. (PW, vol. 12, 18–19)

In any home (except those in poverty), a servant or slave did the dirty work. Since Jesus and the Twelve desired privacy on their last evening together, the steward had dismissed the servants before the guests arrived. Jesus had many times taught His followers that each should be willing to take the lowest place, but on this evening, before the meal, none of the Twelve volunteered.

After the meal, Jesus did not say, "I told you so." He did not growl, "I want to teach you one last lesson." No, Jesus took off His outer clothing. He perceived that He could do this job more easily if He freed himself from clothes that would hinder His movement. Jesus found the jar of water that had been provided for this purpose and washed twenty-four feet.

Jesus Interacted with Peter (John 13:6–11)

The foot-washing story would have been powerful without the Peter detail. Had John omitted these next verses, we never would have known of Peter's gaffe. What might have motivated John to show his friend's foolish humanity once again?

John filled his book with contrasts. We have already noted the contrast between light and darkness and between those who should have taken the lowly role and the One who did. In these verses, John highlighted the contrast between Peter, who hoped to retain control, and Jesus, who "made himself nothing, taking the very nature of a servant" (Phil. 2:7).

WORDS FROM WESLEY
John 13:7

What I do thou knowest not now; but thou shalt know hereafter —
We do not *now know* perfectly any of His works, either of creation, providence, or grace. It is enough that we can love and obey now, and that we shall *know hereafter*. (ENNT)

At this point in the story, Peter likely was incriminating himself by thinking, "I wish I had thought of washing feet before Jesus did. In an upside-down manner, that moment of humility would have been my greatest victory. Jesus might have said something about people remembering me always. And I missed my chance." Perhaps Peter hoped to win the consolation prize by offering to wash his own feet, and perhaps those of Jesus too.

Jesus replied with words that, in effect, said, "Peter, it's too late for that now. I've already begun." John quoted Jesus as saying Peter would **later . . . understand** (13:7) what Jesus was doing.

What and when did Peter later understand? We can't definitively answer this question, but decades later, Peter was undoubtedly remembering this night when he wrote, "Christ suffered for you, leaving you an example, that you should follow in his steps. . . . When they hurled their insults at him, he did not retaliate; when he suffered, he made no threats. Instead, he entrusted himself to him who judges justly" (1 Pet. 2:21, 23).

WORDS FROM WESLEY

John 13:7

One of the earliest principles in the soul of man is a desire of knowledge. . . . Indeed it is this which insensibly leads us on to improve and perfect our reason, which by the present satisfaction it affords encourages us to seek, and renders us capable of receiving instruction. So long as this is restricted within proper bounds, and directed to proper objects, there is not in the mind of man a more delightful or more useful inclination; the pleasures it yields are without number; the field of knowledge hath no end; and in almost every part of it springs up some plant not only gratifying to the eye and cheering to the heart, but useful to the life. The desire of knowledge is a means of attaining to the true wisdom, a means to enlighten the conscience and enlarge the capacity, to lead us to see the all-wise, the all-merciful God in each even of these His lower works. (SCW, 95)

Peter first refused to allow Jesus to touch his feet. When Peter realized that tactic had backfired, he tried the other extreme, hoping somehow to redeem the situation: "Jesus, wash all of me" (see John 13:9). Jesus' response to Peter's request for a bath began on a literal note. "Peter, wouldn't you have washed yourself before you came to tonight's gathering? If so, then the rest of your body is fine. Only your feet need cleaning now" (see v. 10). But then Jesus used the cleanness image to remind Judas of His awareness of the betrayal plot.

Jesus Explained His Actions (John 13:12–17)

After the sermon in action, did the disciples need words? Just in case they did, Jesus spoke. He wanted to ensure that this event served as more than a reminder of His love for them, important as that was. Jesus hoped this encounter would be a long-remembered illustration of words He would speak later that evening: "Love each another as I have loved you" (15:12).

WORDS FROM WESLEY

John 13:14

Ye ought also to wash one another's feet—And why did they not? Why do we not read of any one apostle ever washing the feet of any other? Because they understood the Lord better. They knew He never designed that this should be literally taken. He designed to teach them the great lesson of humble love, as well as to confer inward purity upon them. And hereby He teaches us, 1. In every possible way to assist each other in attaining that purity, 2. To wash each other's feet, by performing all sorts of good offices to each other, even those of the lowest kind, when opportunity serves, and the necessity of any calls for them. (ENNT)

The disciples had correctly recognized who Jesus was: **Teacher** and **Lord** (13:13). He was both instructor and one far superior to them. But as a leader, He "did not come to be served, but to serve, and to give his life as a ransom for many" (Mark 10:45). "As **I . . . have washed your feet, you also should wash one another's feet**" (John 13:14).

Did Jesus intend to establish another sacrament—foot-washing—to accompany baptism and Communion? Some church groups believe so. Whatever Jesus meant, He must have intended His meaning to go beyond teaching mere foot-washing to a broader attitude of true servanthood. "Whoever wants to become great among you must be your servant, and whoever wants to be first must be your slave" (Matt. 20:26–27).

But from the beginning, Jesus knew His church would have little effect if its members sought to be called "servants" without earning the title. Instead, He invited His disciples to follow His example: **"You will be blessed if you do them"**—what He has done (John 13:17).

DISCUSSION

Jesus was ready to observe the Passover Feast that featured a sacrificial lamb. He knew He would die soon as God's sacrificial lamb, but He entertained no self-pity. His thoughts were about serving others. Look for evidence of His selfless service in John 13:1–17.

[handwritten: was so - time to go to the father   Knew from beginning]

1. How do you know from verse 1 that Jesus understood what awaited Him in Jerusalem?

[handwritten margin: 12 tribes or 13 apostles?]
[handwritten: Sacrifice on the cross]

2. What do you find so amazing about Jesus' love for His disciples? For you? *[handwritten: Unconditional   patience, servant]*

3. How does verse 4 add deeper appreciation in you for what Jesus endured on the cross? *[handwritten: Humble   Became a servant to serve us all]*

4. Why do you think Judas was such a willing pawn in Satan's hands? *[handwritten: Never got (Jesus) greedy, committed suicide, not forgiven]*

5. Read 1 Peter 5:8–9. How can a believer resist Satan's temptations? *[handwritten: Self controlled and alert, resist, stand firm in faith   others - similar experiences]*

[handwritten margin: save himself or save the world]

6. How did Jesus show true humility? *[handwritten: - washing feet, servant]*

7. How did Peter show false humility? *[handwritten: tried to cover - should have thru him first]*

8. How can you follow Jesus' example of humility on behalf of fellow believers? *[handwritten: Do good deeds for others, even longest kin(d) when opportunity arises and is necessary]*

[handwritten margin: seek to serve not be served   everyone]

PRAYER

Jesus, thank You for being a humble servant, even though You have power over all things. Help us to follow Your example and love and humbly serve those around us as You served Your disciples.

[handwritten circled: 14]

10

THE HOLY SPIRIT'S ROLE
IN GOD'S REDEMPTION PLAN

John 16:5–16

The Holy Spirit witnesses the truth of the plan ordained by the Father and carried out by the Son.

It's tough to say good-bye. Tears flow down the face of a young wife as she says good-bye to her soldier-husband leaving for service in Afghanistan. Parents choke back their emotions when they leave their son or daughter at a distant college campus for the first time. Tears sting the faces of loved ones gathered for a final farewell at the bedside of a dying parent or grandparent. Yes, it's tough to say good-bye.

When Jesus said good-bye to His disciples, He tempered the sad news with the comforting assurance that He would send the Holy Spirit to them. This study will encourage you to avail yourself of the Holy Spirit's ministry as you long for Jesus' return.

COMMENTARY

Beginning with the previous study, the setting for three studies is Jesus' last meal with His disciples. This supper was eaten immediately before Jesus' arrest, trial, and crucifixion. John gave considerably more detail about this meal than any of the other three gospels (John 13–17). His record also focuses on several details that are different from the other gospels. Many scholars believe John wrote his gospel later than the other three and that he intended to supplement their work.

Most noticeably, John did not record the institution of the Lord's Supper. He did record Jesus' washing of the disciples' feet. Some believers understand John 13:14 as a command that

Christians should practice a ritual of foot-washing. However, most Christians understand Jesus' words and example as calling for all sorts of humble acts of service to each other. John also records extensive sections of discourse that are not found elsewhere: (1) Jesus' words of comfort in chapter 14; (2) the discourse on the true vine in chapter 15; (3) teachings about the coming of the Holy Spirit in chapter 16; and (4) Jesus' prayer for His disciples in chapter 17. As we might expect from John, love is a repeated theme throughout these chapters.

As stated above, this study focuses on the future gift of the Holy Spirit. These verses follow Jesus' discourse on the true vine and His prediction that the world would hate the disciples just as it hated Him, all recorded in John 15. The prediction of opposition continues in chapter 16: "All this I have told you so that you will not go astray. They will put you out of the synagogue; in fact, a time is coming when anyone who kills you will think he is offering a service to God" (16:1). However, Jesus promises that in spite of hatred and opposition, the Spirit of truth would come from the Father to testify about Him and to offer counsel and comfort for believers.

For Your Good, I Am Going Away (John 16:5–7)

"Now I am going to him who sent me, yet none of you asks me, 'Where are you going?'" (v. 5). The background for this statement is found in chapters 13 and 14. Jesus had already discussed His departure from the disciples. Characteristically, Peter wanted to know where Jesus was going (13:36). In reply, Jesus told Peter "Where I am going, you cannot follow now, but you will follow later" (13:36). Already, Jesus had told the disciples that one of them would betray Him and, in a final gesture of friendship, had offered bread to Judas. After Judas received the bread, he had gone out into the night to carry out the betrayal (13:21–30).

Peter spoke up again: "Lord, why can't I follow you now? I will lay down my life for you" (13:37). Jesus then told Peter that, rather than dying for Him, Peter's bravado would vanish and he would deny Jesus three times. Furthermore, that would occur before the rooster crowed the next morning. Clearly the disciples were troubled by the things Jesus was telling them, so Jesus tried to comfort them: "Do not let your hearts be troubled. Trust in God; trust also in me. . . . I am going . . . to prepare a place for you. . . . I will come back and take you to be with me" (14:1–3).

The disciples were also quite confused. "Thomas said to him, 'Lord, we don't know where you are going, so how can we know the way?'" (14:5). And Jesus replied, "I am the way and the truth and the life" (14:6). Philip also expressed frustration in 14:8, and the other Judas did the same in 14:22. Jesus obviously was concerned about the disciples and their welfare, and He continued to reassure them with words of comfort and instruction.

Peter had asked where Jesus was going, but the conversation quickly turned in a different direction (13:36). Thomas had said they did not know where Jesus was going, but he had not asked specifically (14:5). They knew Jesus had said they would be separated from Him, and they were **filled with grief** (16:6). With the ominous tone of the conversation, the disciples were afraid of what would happen to Jesus. No doubt, they were also concerned about their own welfare. The ordeal ahead was frightening even though Jesus promised the outcome would be good. Jesus had predicted His death and had promised He would take up His life again (10:14–18), but most likely the disciples still did not fully understand what was going to happen. The thought of the death of their Lord was dreadful and probably was almost unthinkable for them.

Nevertheless, Jesus' leaving was for their good. **"I tell you the truth: It is for your good that I am going away"** (16:7). He had already told them His going away was for their good in 14:1–3, because He was going to prepare a place for them. This time His promise of a good outcome focuses on the coming of the Holy Spirit: **"Unless I go away, the Counselor will not come to you; but if I go, I will send him to you"** (16:7). In God's plan, the Spirit would not come in His fullness until Jesus had completed His earthly ministry. We can speculate on why God planned events this way, but we cannot say for sure.

Jesus reassured the grieving apostles that His going away was really for their good and would result in the coming of the Counselor. They could not yet appreciate the fact that the constant presence of the Spirit would be all they would need after Jesus was gone.

The Spirit Comes to Convict (John 16:8–11)

"When he comes, he will convict the world of guilt in regard to sin and righteousness and judgment" (v. 8). The Spirit would come to be a Counselor and helper to the disciples, but He would also come to reprove and convict. He would convince men and women as He dealt with their hearts.

WORDS FROM WESLEY
John 16:8

Will convince—All of *the world*—Who do not obstinately resist, by your preaching and miracles, *of sin, and of righteousness, and of judgment*—He who is convinced *of sin*, either accepts the *righteousness* of Christ, or is *judged* with Satan. (ENNT)

"In regard to sin because men do not believe in me" (v. 9). First, the Spirit convicts of sin. The greatest sin is that of unbelief, which prevents God's grace from operating in our hearts. There is no way human effort alone can produce conviction for sin. But the Spirit can make hearts tender and can convince the most hardened unbeliever of his or her sin. The Jews were hardened as they brought Jesus to trial and eventual crucifixion, but their hard hearts were melted when Peter preached to them on the day of Pentecost (Acts 2:37). Hardened sinners whom Christians seemingly cannot touch can be melted to tears of repentance by the convicting power of the Holy Spirit. Those unbelievers who seem beyond reach can be stripped of their defenses and cut to the heart by the convincing work of the Spirit. The Spirit convicts of sin.

WORDS FROM WESLEY

John 16:9

Of sin—Particularly of unbelief, which is the confluence of all sins, and binds them all down upon us. (ENNT)

"In regard to righteousness, because I am going to the Father, where you can see me no longer" (John 16:10). Not only does the Holy Spirit convince us of sin, He also convinces us of the righteousness of Christ, for which all humankind should strive. The Jews are a good example of this fact also. Before the coming of the Spirit, they opposed Jesus and said He was empowered by demons (Matt. 12:24). But the power of the Spirit turned many Jewish opponents into believers. The apostle Paul is a prime illustration of one who persecuted the faith but became convinced of Christ's righteousness (Rom. 3:26). Jesus is no longer present as a living example of true righteousness for humankind to observe, but the Spirit continues to convince of righteousness through the witness of the Word and the witness of believers. The Spirit convinces of righteousness.

"In regard to judgment, because the prince of this world now stands condemned" (John 16:11). The Spirit also brings conviction of judgment. Though many people live sinfully in what seems to be a carefree way, the Spirit brings home the awareness that we will be judged for our sins. We may seem to get by for the present, but the Spirit is faithful to make us aware that we will be judged unless we are forgiven. The prince of this world does his best to deceive us, implying that sin is really good and God is opposed to our happiness (Gen. 3:1–5; 2 Cor. 11:14). But even **the prince of this world** will be judged and **condemned** (John 16:11). The Spirit convicts of judgment.

Jesus listed these three activities as the work of the Spirit in relation to the world. The Holy Spirit alone convinces unbelievers of their need, and the unpleasantness of conviction is another gift of His grace designed to produce the fruit of repentance and faith.

The Spirit Comes to Reveal Truth (John 16:12–13)

Jesus taught the disciples a great deal throughout His ministry on earth. No doubt the Gospels only reveal a small amount of His teaching, but in His incarnate state, He was limited by time and space. He could only do so much within the confines of the temporal order (see John 21:25). Furthermore, the disciples could only handle so much. They did not understand some of what He had already taught them, let alone what would be revealed to them later on.

"I have much more to say to you, more than you can now bear. But when he, the Spirit of truth, comes, he will guide you into all truth" (16:12–13). The Spirit would not be limited by time and space. He would be able to speak truth to all who would listen, and that would continue throughout all time. He would bring to mind the truths the apostles would later record for us in the Gospels and other New Testament Scriptures. He would bring the truth of Christ to the apostles and would also open their minds to understand things they could not yet comprehend. The Spirit would reveal things about Christ that Christ would have said if He had not been limited by time, space, and the comprehension of the disciples.

WORDS FROM WESLEY
John 16:12

I have yet many things to say—Concerning my passion, death, resurrection, and the consequences of it. These things we have, not in uncertain traditions, but in the Acts, the Epistles, and the Revelation. *But you cannot bear them now*—Both because of your littleness of faith, and your immoderate sorrow. (ENNT)

The Spirit of truth has guided believers into all truth down through church history. What a blessing that He continues to guide us into truth today. While there have been theological disagreements and even heresy, church leaders have faithfully studied the Scriptures and prayed for guidance, basic agreement generally has come regarding the major doctrines. **The Spirit of truth . . . will guide you into all truth** (v. 13).

The Spirit Comes to Bring Glory to Christ (John 16:14–16)

The Holy Spirit comes to bring honor to Christ. **"He will bring glory to me by taking from what is mine and making it known to you"** (v. 14). The third person of the Trinity does not glorify himself; His work is totally devoted to lifting up Christ and His work of redemption. He glorifies Christ by revealing things about Him. The disciples could only understand partial truth while Jesus was with them. The Spirit would open up new truths about Jesus to their minds as they were able to comprehend them.

"All that belongs to the Father is mine. That is why I said the Spirit will take from what is mine and make it known to you" (v. 15). All truth is in God and thus belongs to Jesus. Furthermore, Jesus claimed to literally be the truth (14:6). Paul said in Him "are hidden all the treasures of wisdom and knowledge" (Col. 2:3). When the Spirit reveals truth, He reveals Jesus and the

Father. He simply takes from the truth of Jesus and passes it on to us. In a sense, we can only understand the Bible as the Spirit reveals it to us. New insights and understanding come through His faithful ministry to us.

"In a little while you will see me no more, and then after a little while you will see me" (John 16:16). The disciples were sad that Jesus was going away. In retrospect, these promises related to the Spirit's coming and His work for believers made it plain that the disciples would benefit greatly from God's plan. But losing Jesus seemed overwhelming to them at that time. On the day of Pentecost, they would begin to realize the truth of the promises. They would see Jesus again, both in His resurrection body and through new insight and understanding through the gracious work of the Holy Spirit.

DISCUSSION

The disciples spent more than three years with Jesus, but that close relationship was about to end. Jesus would soon leave them, but He would send the Holy Spirit to them. As you study John 16:5–16, look for ways the Holy Spirit would minister to the disciples.

1. Jesus promised to send the Counselor to the disciples. Why is this an appropriate name for the Holy Spirit?

2. What connection do you see between the Spirit's presence in believers and His convicting the world?

3. How does the convicting ministry of the Holy Spirit affect your willingness to share the gospel?

4. Why do you agree or disagree that Satan's condemnation is a present reality?

5. Read Revelation 20:10. Describe Satan's final abode.

6. Compare John 16:13–15 and 2 Timothy 3:16. How would you describe the Spirit's role in giving us God's Word?

7. How has the Holy Spirit helped you understand Scripture?

8. Jesus told the disciples they would see Him again. Why are you most desirous of seeing Jesus?

PRAYER

Lord, thank You for sending the Holy Spirit. Thank You for guiding us to the truth of the gospel by the Spirit, for convicting us of our guilt, and for comforting us in the face of opposition. Help us continue to be open to Your Spirit's guidance in the truth.

11

OVERCOMING THE WORLD

John 17:1–21

Loving Christ fully is the convincing way to attract
unbelievers to Him and His church.

Don't look for the Lord's Prayer in public schools. It is no
longer there. But you can find it in John 17. It isn't the prayer
most Christians refer to as the Lord's Prayer, the one that begins,
"Our Father, who art in heaven"; it is the one our Lord prayed
for all believers. He asked the Father to protect us, fill us with
joy, unite us, and sanctify us.

You may know that other believers are praying for you, and their
prayers encourage you. But how much greater encouragement
can you derive by knowing Jesus prayed for you before He
embraced the cross? This study will encourage and strengthen
you to represent the Lord in a sinful world.

COMMENTARY

This study is the third in the series taken from John's account
of the Last Supper Jesus had with His disciples just before His
betrayal. Here we focus on Jesus' prayer for His disciples and for
all who would later "believe in [Him]" (17:20). The setting leading
up to this prayer may assist our understanding of the prayer itself.

The previous study ended with Jesus' statement: "In a little while
you will see me no more, and then after a little while you will see
me" (16:16). This statement and another about "going to the
Father" (16:10) puzzled the disciples. "What does he mean . . . ?
We don't understand what he is saying" (16:17–18). Jesus saw
that they were puzzled, and He was also concerned about them

as the crisis of His arrest and crucifixion unfolded. Thus, Jesus gave further explanation of His statements, which John recorded in the latter part of chapter 16.

Jesus continued: "I tell you the truth, you will weep and mourn while the world rejoices. You will grieve, but your grief will turn to joy" (16:20). Like a mother in in pain during childbirth, their pain and grief would be short-lived (16:21–22). Jesus would no longer be present to receive their requests, but His "Father will give you whatever you ask in my name" (16:23). And at the coming of the Holy Spirit, they would not be left alone (16:7). Soon (apparently after the resurrection) He would speak to them plainly rather than through the figurative language He had been using (16:25).

The disciples finally seemed to understand (16:29–30) when Jesus told them, "I came from the Father and entered the world; now I am leaving the world and going back to the Father" (16:28). Still, Jesus knew the disciples would be confused and scattered as the events of the next day unfolded. They would leave Him alone, without human companions, but the Father would be with Him (16:31–32). Before praying, Jesus' last words of encouragement were "I have told you these things, so that in me you may have peace. In this world you will have trouble. But take heart! I have overcome the world" (16:33). Thus, Jesus led into His great prayer for His disciples.

Glorify Your Son (John 17:1–5)

"Father, the time has come. Glorify your Son, that your Son may glorify you" (v. 1). Jesus' work on earth was almost complete. The time of His ultimate humiliation and death was imminent. John did not record Jesus' prayer in the garden of Gethsemane where, if it could be the Father's will, He prayed for deliverance (Luke 22:39–44). Here, Jesus was with His eleven remaining disciples as He prayed, and He prayed that God would glorify Him and thereby also receive glory. The final humiliation of Christ was His death, but, Paul told us, that humiliation led to His supreme exaltation "and gave him the name that is above every name" (Phil. 2:9). God would transform the worst event of human history into the greatest triumph of all. Jesus would be glorified, and through His obedience, He would bring glory to His Father.

How is God glorified by us? One commentator notes that God receives glory when we are obedient. Jesus obeyed fully: "He humbled himself and became obedient to death—even death on a cross!" (Phil. 2:8; compare Heb. 10:5–10). When Jesus prayed that the Son would be glorified and that the Father would be glorified in the Son, He was implicitly praying for the courage and strength to obey even to death.

God is glorified when hearers are obedient by believing. **For you granted him authority over all people that he might give eternal life to all those you have given him** (John 17:2). Christ's work was universal in scope, and His authority extended over all believers. Eternal life comes to all who **know you, the only true God, and Jesus Christ, whom you have sent** (v. 3).

WORDS FROM WESLEY
John 17:3

To know—By loving holy faith, *thee the only true God*—The only cause and end of all things; not excluding the Son and the Holy Ghost, no more than the Father is excluded from being Lord, 1 Cor. 8:6 but the false gods of the heathens, *and Jesus Christ*—As their prophet, priest, and king: *this is life eternal*—It is both the way to, and the essence of, everlasting happiness. (ENNT)

Christ's work with the disciples was almost complete; only eleven had become believers. But Jesus was not discouraged. **"I have brought you glory on earth by completing the work**

you gave me to do" (v. 4). From a human perspective, the outlook for Jesus and His followers was not encouraging. The leader would die on a Roman cross the next day.

There were only eleven faithful disciples plus a few additional adherents. Even the eleven would be scattered, looking out for themselves as best they could. Their world that centered on Jesus seemed to be falling apart. But God was in control, and His plan was being accomplished even as things seemed to be collapsing. "But God chose the foolish things of the world to shame the wise; God chose the weak things of the world to shame the strong" (1 Cor. 1:27). Jesus knew the Father was being glorified and that the Father's will was being done despite the dismal prospect from the human outlook.

Taking the divine perspective, Jesus prayed on. **"And now, Father, glorify me in your presence with the glory I had with you before the world began"** (John 17:5). His humiliation was not yet complete, but after that humiliation, Jesus would return to the Father's presence in triumph. His glory would be restored to be as it was before the world began. Surely this prospect helped Jesus face and endure the terrible events of the next twenty-four hours. He "for the joy set before him endured the cross, scorning its shame, and sat down at the right hand of the throne of God" (Heb. 12:2).

Keep and Protect Those You Have Given Me (John 17:6–12)

Jesus next prayed for the eleven. **"I have revealed you to those whom you gave me out of the world. They were yours; you gave them to me and they have obeyed your word"** (v. 6). The disciples were few in number, but they were obedient. Thus, God could use them. They had heard Jesus' teaching, and they believed it. **"They knew with certainty that I came from you, and they believed that you sent me"** (v. 8). These few men had faith, and God would give them the strength for whatever lay ahead in spite of what seemed to be overwhelming odds.

Jesus was very concerned for the future protection of the eleven disciples after He was gone. **"I pray for them. I am not praying for the world, but for those you have given me, for they are yours"** (v. 9). Everything Jesus had belonged to the Father, including His disciples. The disciples had brought glory to Jesus, which in turn brought glory to the Father (v. 10). **"I will remain in the world no longer, but they are still in the world, and I am coming to you. Holy Father, protect them by the power of your name . . . so that they may be one as we are one"** (v. 11). The disciples needed protection that God alone could provide. Protection for the disciples was also tied to their unity. God's purposes on earth are evidently hindered when His people are divided.

WORDS FROM WESLEY

John 17:10

All things that are mine are thine, and that are thine are mine— These are very high and strong expressions, too grand for any mere creature to use; as implying that all things whatsoever, inclusive of the divine nature, perfections, and operations, are the common property of the Father and the Son. And this is the original ground of that peculiar property, which both the Father and the Son have in the persons who were given to Christ as Mediator; according to what is said in the close of the verse, of His being *glorified by them;* namely, believing in Him, and so acknowledging His glory. (ENNT)

Jesus had said all He could to reassure the disciples (see chs. 13–16). While He was with them, He **"protected them and kept them safe by that name you gave me"** (v. 12). Now He prayed for them that the Father would continue that protection and do it through the power of the name the Father had given Jesus. Only Judas Iscariot had rejected the protection of Jesus' name and had been lost from the Twelve. Judas was doomed for destruction, not because God had predestined his awful choice, but because God foreknew what Judas would choose. He would betray Jesus.

WORDS FROM WESLEY

John 17:11

Great stress has been laid upon this text; and it has been hence inferred, that all those whom the Father had given him (a phrase frequently occurring in this chapter) must infallibly persevere to the end.

And yet, in the very next verse, our Lord himself declares that one of those whom the Father had given him did not persevere unto the end, but perished everlastingly. (WJW, vol. 10, 292)

Make Their Joy Full (John 17:13–19)

That Jesus knew the disciples were very troubled at the prospect of His death and the uncertainty of the future is evident from 14:1. Jesus, too, was deeply troubled, but He also saw the joy ahead as He completed His work of redemption. Now He prayed that the disciples also would **have the full measure of His joy within them** (17:13). They had the Father's word that Jesus had given them (v. 14), and that was certainly a strength. But there was also a negative side: **the world has hated them, for they are not of the world any more than** Jesus was **of the world** (v. 14). They were living in a dangerous world that was an ongoing threat to them, a world, in fact, that was about to kill their Master.

"My prayer is not that you take them out of the world but that you protect them from the evil one" (v. 15). The work to which the disciples were called was in the world, so Jesus did not want them to be removed from the world. His prayer was for their protection—from the evil in the world and especially from the Evil One at work in the world. The disciples did not fit into the world any more than Jesus did (v. 16). They would always be aliens while they remained in the world. But Jesus prayed that they would be kept from harm. Christians who fit comfortably into the world's structure are hardly following the examples set by the disciples and their Lord.

Sanctify them by the truth; your word is truth (v. 17). The Greek word used here is often translated **sanctify**. It means "to set apart" or "to make holy." We may understand Jesus' prayer to involve both meanings. If so, He prayed that the disciples would be set apart for the work to which they were called and that they would be made holy. The Father had sent Jesus into the world, and now Jesus was sending the disciples into the world to complete the work He had begun (v. 18). He set himself apart for His work so they might also be set apart for continuing that work.

The work to which the disciples were appointed was difficult; the world would hate them and oppose them. With such prospects, was it possible that disciples could be full of joy? Indeed, it was possible for four reasons: (1) They could rest in the confidence that their Lord had prayed for their protection; (2) they could know they were living in an alien world, but that world desperately needed their message; (3) they could know their mission into the world was the most important mission people had ever undertaken; and (4) they could know God had set them apart for the task to which they were appointed. Joy would come to them without them having to seek it.

WORDS FROM WESLEY

John 17:19

I sanctify myself—I devote myself as a victim, to be sacrificed. (ENNT)

Overcoming the World

Unite All Future Believers as One (John 17:20–21)

Finally, Jesus prayed for all believers. **"My prayer is not for them alone. I pray also for those who will believe in me through their message"** (v. 20). If we are believers in Jesus, He prayed for each of us. Jesus was not only concerned about His eleven disciples gathered with Him that night; He was also concerned about us today. He prayed for us.

What did Jesus pray? **"That all of them may be one, Father, just as you are in me and I am in you. May they also be in us so that the world may believe that you have sent me"** (v. 21). Surely this prayer by our Lord is a strong impetus for Christian unity. Disunity and division among Christians has hindered the spread of the gospel many times, discouraging belief in Jesus. Verse 21 implicitly says disunity would hinder the acceptance of the gospel. Some Christians believe Jesus was praying for unity within one organized church. Thus, they have worked to unite all Christians in one body. How should we understand the unity Jesus prayed for? Surely it is primarily the unity of love. "By this all men will know that you are my disciples, if you love one another" (13:35). Bickering and animosity among Christians disrupts their most important work, that of winning others who need to know Jesus too.

We can be sure Jesus prayed for believers to be one. We can also be sure that since the most important aspect of unity is love, Jesus prayed that we would love one another. John assuredly understood that message and was later known as the apostle of love. It seems clear that believers today can help fulfill Jesus' prayer by loving each other. May it be! Amen!

105

DISCUSSION

[handwritten: GLORIFY / SANCTIFY]

John 17 records what may truly be called the Lord's Prayer.
Find at least three requests Jesus offered to the Father in verses
1–21. *[handwritten: DOING HIS WORK - THAT HE WAS GIVEN TO DO]*

1. How would the Father glorify His Son? How would the
Son glorify His Father? *[handwritten: BY TAKING TO RIGHTFUL PLACE IN HEAVEN]*

2. How does verse 3 define eternal life? Why do you suppose *[handwritten: TO KNOWING / BY FULL MY]*
so many individuals try to find eternal life by religious good *[handwritten: COMMANDS]*
works instead of by knowing Jesus as Savior? *[handwritten: FOR ETERNAL LIFE]*

3. In verse 2, Jesus referred to believers as God's gift to Him.
How does knowing this fact affect the way you live? *[handwritten: HUMBLE - WE ARE GIFTS FROM GOD]*

4. How does verse 5 declare Jesus' eternal existence? His
preeminence? *[handwritten: BEFORE THE WORLD BEGAN]*

5. In what sense are believers "in the world" (v. 11) but not
"of the world" (v. 14)? *[handwritten: RELATIONSHIP WITH JESUS FOCUSED ON ETERNITY]*

6. How is it possible to have joy while living in a hostile world?

7. Why did Jesus leave His disciples—and us—in the world
(see v. 18)? *[handwritten: SPREAD GOOD NEWS THROUGH SALVATION IN CHRIST]*

8. Knowing that the Word plays a vital role in making you
holy, how will you honor it this week?

PRAYER

[handwritten: THE WORD]

Father, thank You for sending Jesus into the world for the sake
of Your glory and our salvation. Jesus, thank You for sending Your
disciples into the world as Your witnesses to spread the gospel.
Help us all to love each other and passionately pursue unity.

[handwritten: PRAY THIS WAY: IN OUR FATHER]

[handwritten: A = D / D - A]

[handwritten: 3 IN 1]

12

THE SIGNIFICANCE OF THE CROSS

John 19:16–37

The cross is the very foundation of all we believe
about God and who we are in Christ.

From the deck of the aircraft carrier USS *Abraham Lincoln*, President Bush announced in 2003, "Mission accomplished." He was referring to the completion of Operation Iraqi Freedom. However, we all know the mission to free Iraq had just begun in 2003. Since 2003, thousands of military men and women have given their lives for the cause of freedom. But when Jesus cried out from the cross, "It is finished," His words truly announced, "Mission accomplished." His death procured our full redemption and gained our freedom from sin and Satan.

You will live in spiritual freedom as you appropriate this study's liberating truth that Jesus paid it all.

COMMENTARY

To the casual reader or the uninformed, the events in these verses all seem rather ordinary. After three years of public ministry, Jesus had finally so agitated the religious leaders, threatening their authority as well as their theological understanding, that they had Him hastily tried and mercilessly crucified for blasphemy. He had, after all, claimed equality with God the Father (see John 5:18; 8:58; 10:30–33), a claim any pious Jew would repudiate. What began the preceding week as a triumphal entry into Jerusalem ended in the humiliation of death. Jesus was born, lived, and died—all very ordinary, human events. Except for one thing: Jesus was God.

What was difficult to see beyond the ordinary events of yet another Roman crucifixion was the fact that something extraordinary was happening. It was not a common criminal on the cross—it was Jesus, the sinless God-Man. He who was part of the Godhead, the Holy Trinity, was willingly laying down His life to pay the penalty for sin.

In John's gospel, the apostle attempts to show his Greek readers the heavenly realities behind the earthly events. He doesn't describe every detail of the crucifixion, knowing full well they are included in the other gospel accounts, but he supplements what is already common knowledge and relates those events that particularly impressed on him the tremendous significance of the death of Christ.

The Setting Leading to the Crucifixion (John 19:16)

The story of Pilate's involvement in the trial and crucifixion of Jesus is recounted in John 18:28 — 19:16. According to Luke 23:7, Pilate sent Jesus to Herod for judgment, and it was Herod's soldiers who mocked Jesus by dressing Him in a royal robe and crown of thorns (compare Luke 23:11; John 19:2–3) before returning Jesus to Pilate. Because the Jewish Sanhedrin had limited rights to impose the death penalty, they had handed over Jesus to the Roman authorities. (Pontius Pilate was the Roman governor of Judea from A.D. 26 to 36.) Three times in this encounter, it is stated that the Jews had "handed over" Jesus (18:30, 35; 19:11). Now it was **Pilate** who **handed** over Jesus **to them** (v. 16). Given the context, the reference is certainly to the Jewish leaders (His accusers), not to Pilate's own **soldiers**. Deuteronomy 17:7 stipulated that it was the accusers who were to be the executioners. The obvious implication of the passage is that although the Roman soldiers took charge of Jesus and performed the act of execution, Jesus had actually been handed over to the will of His own people, who were the real executioners (see John 19:11; Luke 23:25).

The curious thing about John 19:16 is the fact that Pilate handed over Jesus to them at all. Three times Pilate stated that he had found no basis for charges against Jesus (18:38; 19:4, 6), and neither had Herod (Luke 23:15). John said Pilate even "tried to set Jesus free" (19:12). Pilate was certainly not noted for appeasing the Jews, but perhaps he grew tired of the situation and realized the hostile crowd would never relent. How tragic when a man compromises his convictions because he fears people more than God!

The Crucifixion of Jesus (John 19:17–18)

Like Isaac carried the wood for his own sacrifice on Mount Moriah (Gen. 22), Jesus now carried the cross on which He would be crucified—sacrificed for the sins of the world. He had taught His disciples the spiritual ramifications of the cross (Matt. 10:38; 16:24; Mark 8:34; Luke 9:23; 14:27); now He illustrated it literally. But the other three gospels all record that Simon from Cyrene carried the cross for Jesus (Matt. 27:32; Mark 15:21; Luke 23:26), making no mention of Jesus actually carrying it himself. Some merely discount John's version of the story. Others reconcile the accounts by stating that Jesus was too weak to continue because of the flogging, and so Simon was enlisted en route. But to argue over whether or not Jesus ever physically carried **his own cross** (John 19:17) is to miss the point entirely.

WORDS FROM WESLEY

John 19:17

Bearing his cross—Not the whole cross, (for that was too large and heavy) but the transverse beam of it, to which His hands were afterward fastened. This they used to make the person to be executed carry. (ENNT)

John's point is that Jesus carried His own cross: He willingly laid down His own life and "became obedient to death—even death on a cross!" (Phil. 2:8). Willing, self-sacrificing, self-denying obedience is the essence of carrying one's cross, the obligation of every Christian. Jesus' determination to obey God's will and His willingness to take on our sin is the ultimate example of carrying a cross.

The actual location of the crucifixion is unknown; we know only that it was outside the city (19:20; Heb. 13:12). It may have been known as **the place of the Skull** (John 19:17) because of the executions that took place there or because it was located on a hill shaped like a skull.

John did not go into detail about the horror of crucifixion. It was a humiliating form of execution reserved for the basest of criminals. Being crucified as a common criminal along with **two others** (v. 18) only added to the shame: He "was numbered with the transgressors" (Isa. 53:12). With nails through His hands (or wrists, which were considered part of the hand) and feet, Jesus hung on a cross to die as a public spectacle.

The Sign Identifying Jesus (John 19:19–22)

A notice of the crime for which a person was being executed was often placed above his head on the cross. Pilate's inscription was further attestation that there was "no basis for a charge against him" (19:6). There was no crime for which Jesus was being killed; He was killed for who He was. In Pilate's earlier examination of Jesus, he had discovered Jesus to be a king (18:37) and taunted the Jews with the fact several times (18:39; 19:5, 14–15). Some commentators believe Pilate truly came to believe that Jesus was THE KING OF THE JEWS (v. 19), while others think this was continued mockery.

Those who had fought against the Roman oppression claiming God as their King now had chosen Caesar over God's Anointed

One. But whom they chose as king did not alter the fact of who was really their King. The notice was true, whether or not Pilate actually knew it. Once pronounced, Roman law forbade a sentence to be changed, hence Pilate's answer: **What I have written, I have written** (v. 22). So, too, Jesus' kingship was unalterable.

John's gospel alone tells us that the inscription was written in three different languages: **Aramaic**, the common language of the people; **Latin**, the language of law and government; and **Greek**, the language of culture (v. 20). Because the population of Jerusalem had swelled for the Passover Feast, many pilgrims would have come out to witness the execution and read the inscription. Jesus' kingship was proclaimed in the three most widely known languages so everyone would understand and take the proclamation back to their homelands.

The Soldiers at the Cross (John 19:23–24)

Four soldiers witnessed the execution, and, as was customary, they divided up the clothing of their prisoners, leaving them shamefully naked. Some have made much of the fact that Jesus' undergarment was seamless, drawing the parallel between that and the priest's seamless tunic. Here Jesus was acting as High Priest, offering the sacrifice for the sin of the world. But John seemed particularly fascinated with the fact that these greedy soldiers were unconsciously fulfilling prophecy they had probably never even heard (Ps. 22:18). Jesus' crucifixion wasn't some glitch in God's plan, some grand mistake. Everything happened just as God had predicted through His prophets. The crucifixion is precisely why Christ was sent; it was God's plan from the beginning.

WORDS FROM WESLEY
John 19:24

They parted my garments among them—No circumstance of David's life bore any resemblance to this, or to several other passages in [Psalm 22]. So that in this Scripture, as in some others, the prophet [David] seems to have been thrown into a preternatural ecstasy, wherein, personating the Messiah, he spoke barely what the Spirit dictated, without any regard to himself. (ENNT)

Jesus' Followers at the Foot of the Cross (John 19:25–27)

How interesting that, of all the disciples, only John remained with Jesus throughout the crucifixion. Perhaps the others were too frightened, disillusioned, or ashamed to watch their Lord die such a humiliating death. But four brave and devoted women, including His mother, were there keeping vigil.

It was Jesus' greatest moment of anguish, and yet He was still filled with compassion for others. At the hour of death, He carefully and lovingly made provision for His earthly mother. He entrusted His mother to the care of His beloved disciple, not to His half-brothers, underscoring the fact that the Christian bond is far greater than that of blood relationship. The commentator Adam Clarke speculated that the reason John was the only disciple who died a natural death was because of his responsibility to take care of Mary; God spared her whose heart had already been pierced as with a sword (Luke 2:35) from any further tragedy.

The Final Moments of Jesus' Earthly Life (John 19:28–30)

So that the Scripture would be fulfilled, Jesus said, "I am thirsty" (v. 28). The meaning here is not that Jesus merely spoke the words to fulfill Scripture, but that He was honestly thirsty (one of the effects of crucifixion) and that God's will revealed in Old Testament prophecy was finding expression. **Wine vinegar**

(v. 29), or sour wine, the common drink of the Roman soldiers, was offered to Jesus to refresh Him. This shouldn't be confused with the intoxicating wine mixed with myrrh or frankincense to deaden pain that was offered and refused earlier (Matt. 27:34; Mark 15:23). Jesus received the refreshment, which revived Him enough to utter His final words in John 19:30.

Jesus had come for one divine purpose: to give His life as a ransom for many. He suffered, bled, and died in our place to bring forgiveness for sin and reconciliation to God. At the very moment He died, it was all finished. The debt of sin was paid; God's plan was finished; His justice was satisfied; prophecy was fulfilled; Christ's job was done. It was not a cry of defeat, but of ultimate victory (Col. 2:15). No one took Jesus' life from Him; He himself gave it up willingly (John 10:18). In the moment of death, the serpent's head was crushed (Gen. 3:15) and the kingdom of God inaugurated. The battle was over.

Jesus' Bones Not Broken on the Cross (John 19:31–37)

Jesus was crucified on Friday, the day of preparation for the Sabbath. The next day was a special Sabbath because it came during the Passover celebration. By breaking the legs of the victims, death would be hastened, allowing the Jews to keep their law and attend their ceremonies without further delay. Since Jesus was already dead, His legs weren't broken. During Passover, the Jews would celebrate God's deliverance of His people from slavery in Egypt and His miraculous provision, through the blood of a lamb, for the lives of their firstborn to be spared (see Ex. 12). The Jews were in a hurry to rush off to their Passover celebration, not realizing that the Passover Lamb had already been slain.

WORDS FROM WESLEY

John 19:36

A bone of it shall not be broken—This was originally spoken of the paschal lamb, an eminent type of Christ. (ENNT)

Doctors and theologians alike have speculated on the miraculous flow of blood and water from Jesus' side. Some see in this symbolism of the Eucharist (Communion) and water baptism. Others identify the blood and water with the old and new covenants or with justification and sanctification. Some believe it showed the twofold power of redemption through redemptive blood and living water. John's primary purpose seems not to report a miracle, but to give absolute proof of Jesus' death. Without the reality of death, the miracle of the resurrection in the next chapter would be nullified. He gave emphatic testimony that this is true, though scholars disagree over whether the man who saw it is John himself, a soldier, or some other man. John emphasized again the miraculous nature of the fulfillment of yet another prophecy, further proof that Jesus was—and is—truly the Son of God.

WORDS FROM WESLEY

John 19:37

They shall look on him whom they have pierced—He was *pierced* by the soldier's spear. They who have occasioned His sufferings by their sins (and who has not?) *shall* either *look upon him* in this world with penitential sorrow: or with terror, when He cometh in the clouds of heaven. (ENNT)

DISCUSSION

As you read John 19:16–37, see who was involved in the crucifixion, but keep in mind that Jesus' death was voluntary. Notice especially His statement in verse 30: "It is finished." He had completed His mission to redeem us.

[handwritten: Common or Crucifiction]

1. Why do you think Jesus was crucified at Golgotha, a location meaning "the place of the Skull"?

2. How would you describe Pilate's character? *[handwritten: A PLEASER]*

3. Why do you think Pilate identified Jesus as "KING OF THE JEWS"? *[handwritten: HE BELIEVED IT AND HE MOCKED THE JEWS]*

4. Why do you think Pilate refused to change what the sign announced? *[handwritten: HE BELIEVED IT — ONCE WRITTEN NEVER CHANGED) common PRATICE]*

5. Read Psalm 22 and list the prophecies Jesus fulfilled when He died on the cross. *[handwritten: CROSS, CASTING CLOTHING, BONES IN TACT DELIVER ME, WHY HAVE YOU ABANDED ME]*

6. What significance do you attach to the fact that Jesus gave John the task of caring for Mary? *[handwritten: LOVED HIM ALL ONE FAMILY]*

7. The Greek word for "It is finished" can be translated "Paid in full." What did Jesus pay in full on the cross? *[handwritten: SINS OF HUMANITY RESTORED]*

8. Read Exodus 12:46. Why is it significant that none of Jesus' bones were broken? *[handwritten: REGULATIONS OF PASSOVER SACRAFICIAL LAMB SAME TIME AS JESUS DEATH]*

PRAYER

Lord, You made the ultimate sacrifice for us, though we have done nothing to deserve it. Thank You for enduring unspeakable torture and pain, even taking on sin and death, as the ultimate sacrifice to open the way for us to be restored and cleansed.

[handwritten: ONLY ONE WHO DIED A NATURAL DEATH]

[handwritten: REPHLACEMENT THEOLOGY]

[handwritten circled: 16]

13

THE MEANING OF THE RESURRECTION

John 20:1–18, 30–31

The indisputable fact of Christ's resurrection becomes the
convincing argument for the gospel message.

It is never pleasant to learn that a store or restaurant has gone
out of business, but if Jesus had not risen from the dead,
churches might just as well hang an "Out of Business" sign on
their doors. They would have nothing to offer anyone—no good
news of salvation, no reason to pray, no possibility of joy and
peace, no power for living, and no hope of eternity. But Jesus
did rise from the dead, and church doors are open for business.
They let us in to be edified and let us out to share the message
of the resurrection with the whole world.

This study will motivate you to joyfully serve the living Savior.

COMMENTARY

Several times during Jesus' ministry, He prophesied His
coming death and resurrection (Matt. 12:40; 16:21; 17:23; 20:19;
John 2:19; 10:17–18). Though His disciples were slow to understand,
Jesus' enemies certainly remembered His prediction. After Joseph
of Arimathea and Nicodemus removed Jesus' body from the cross,
anointed Him with burial spices, and placed Him in a new garden
tomb, the chief priests and Pharisees urged Pilate to post a guard
until the third day to ensure Jesus' disciples wouldn't steal the body,
claiming He had risen as He said (Matt. 27:62–66).

Jesus was dead and buried. A large stone lay in front of the
tomb. The stone was sealed with a Roman seal and a guard kept
watch. If it was a Roman guard of four men, they would have

been highly trained and heavily armed. If it was a temple guard, falling asleep while on duty would have been punishable by death. All indications were that no one could secretly steal away the body of Jesus. He was there to stay . . . or so they thought!

It is in Matthew that we learn about an early morning earthquake and an angel rolling away the stone—not to let Jesus out, but to let others see that He was already gone. The stunned guards were paralyzed by their fear. After reporting the event to the chief priests, they were paid to claim the disciples had stolen the body while they were sleeping—an absurdity given the facts. If they were sleeping, how could they possibly know who stole the body? How could they not be awakened by the commotion? Why weren't they being punished for serious dereliction of duty?

The importance of the resurrection cannot be overestimated. In 1 Corinthians 15:17 and 19, Paul said, "And if Christ has not been raised, your faith is futile; you are still in your sins. . . . If only for this life we have hope in Christ, we are to be pitied more than all men." All of Jesus' claims to be the only way to the Father, to be one with God, to be the means of eternal life, are meaningless without the resurrection. There would be no victory, no hope. Had the story of Christ ended with the crucifixion, it would have been dramatic, but final. Jesus would have joined the ranks of martyrs, but His influence would have been limited to that of a prophet or teacher. Thankfully, the story doesn't end with Jesus' death on a cross. As we see in John 20, the grave could not hold Him and death was swallowed up in victory.

Finding the Tomb Empty (John 20:1–9)

It was Sunday morning when these events took place—the third day. By Jewish reckoning, any portion of a day (which was measured from sunset to sunset) was counted as a day. Since Jesus was placed in the tomb on Friday before sunset, Friday was counted as the first day; Saturday, the second; and the portion from sunset Saturday to Sunday morning prior to the rolling away of the stone, the third. **Mary Magdalene** alone is mentioned by John as going **to the tomb**, and she left **while it was still dark** (v. 1). Matthew mentioned two women who left at dawn; Mark noted three women who arrived after sunrise; and Luke mentioned three by name but adds that there were others (Luke 24:10). John was only concerned with Mary and saw no need to mention the others, but it is evident Mary was not alone from her use of the word **we** in 20:2. John's reference to it still being dark when Mary left may not be a contradiction at all. John could be referring to the time the women departed, and in Mark as the time they arrived, or Mary may have arrived earlier than the rest. It still seemed dark simply because, as far as the women knew, Jesus was still dead. The pain and sorrow had not yet been turned into joy.

Mary and the others were visiting the tomb with spices to anoint Jesus' body (Mark 16:1; Luke 24:1). Apparently they had given no thought as to how they would move the stone to accomplish this, but they were driven by devotion to at least try. When they found the grave empty, Mary immediately ran to tell Peter and John. It is curious that John quoted Mary as saying, **"They have taken the Lord"** (20:2), when according to the other gospels, she had already been told by an angel that Jesus had risen from the dead. Maybe in all the confusion, that is all she said— or maybe that's all the disciples heard. It's also possible that Mary left to tell the disciples the body was missing before seeing any angel. The other women would have remained and experienced the proclamation of the angel but would have left to tell the good news before Peter and John arrived. This would explain why Mary appeared to be so forlorn (and alone) in the following verses and why the thought of a resurrection had not yet occurred to her.

The fact that the disciples ran to the tomb, an indication of strong emotion and urgency, is evidence that they had no part in a conspiracy to steal Jesus' body as the soldiers claimed. Had they stolen the body while the guard slept, they would have taken their time getting to the tomb, since they would have already been aware of what they would find.

It is obvious from this description that John was indeed giving us an eyewitness account of what happened, offering detailed information (such as who arrived at the tomb first and who went in first) that seems of little importance to the plot of the story. John may have been reluctant to enter the tomb because of the Mosaic prohibitions of coming into contact with a dead body. The impetuous Peter had no such reservations, especially since Mary had already told him the body was not there. The arrangement of the grave clothes seemed sufficient evidence to cause John to believe Jesus had risen from the dead, even though he didn't yet understand that Scripture pointed to it or that it was an integral part of God's plan. The burial cloth that had been placed around Jesus' head was separate from the linen. It may have appeared as if Jesus' body had simply evaporated, leaving the wrappings untouched in their previous position. Robbers would not have taken time to arrange the grave clothes in such a manner; they would have stolen the body grave clothes and all.

WORDS FROM WESLEY

John 20:8

He saw—That the body was not there, *and believed*—That they had taken it away as Mary said. (ENNT)

Mary's Despair (John 20:10–15)

Peter and John returned to the homes they were staying in while in Jerusalem, but Mary chose to stay near the tomb, wailing in grief. It is obvious that, even at this point, she still had no idea

Christ had risen. You would think the appearance of two angels would immediately signal that something miraculous had happened and spark hope. But Mary only repeated what she had told the disciples: Someone had taken Jesus' body, and she didn't know where they had put Him. Perhaps she thought Joseph of Arimathea and Nicodemus had planned this to be only a temporary burial place and had taken Jesus after the Sabbath to another tomb. Or maybe she conjectured that friends or other disciples had moved Him. She did not seem to notice that they were angels, possibly because of her tears or her preoccupation with the whereabouts of Jesus' body.

Sometimes we look at Mary in amazement and wonder how she could not recognize Jesus. Since John 20:16 mentions that she turned toward Him when He spoke her name, it is possible that here she had just turned momentarily, long enough to discern the figure of a man, then returned to look at the angels or to continue grieving. But it could be that she was just unprepared to recognize Him. She wasn't expecting Him. Doubt, despair, and preoccupation with our problems often keep us from recognizing Jesus' presence. In all fairness to Mary, Jesus may have had an altered appearance, either because of the flogging He received prior to His crucifixion or because of His divine state. Later, when He appeared to two men on the Emmaus road, they didn't recognize Him either, even though their hearts burned within them as He taught them from the Scriptures. "They were kept from recognizing him" (Luke 24:16, 32).

Mary assumed the man was the gardener who would have overseen the care of the tombs. Surely he would have known if someone had been moving bodies. Mary's devotion and love for Jesus here are so apparent. She wanted to know where His body was so she could go get it—without any thought as to how she would move the body by herself. That didn't matter to her. He was her Lord. She would work out the details after she found Him.

Mary's Encounter with the Risen Christ (John 20:16–18)

Of all the friends and disciples, Mary was the first to see the risen Lord. Maybe it was because she was the most grief-stricken or most in need of His presence. Or maybe it was because she was the only one who waited long enough. She was persistently devoted and refused to leave the garden until she had found Him. Christ comes to those who wait on Him (Isa. 40:31); God answers the prayers of the persistent (Luke 18:1–8).

At the mention of her name, Mary's eyes were opened and she recognized the One who had been her Teacher. It is highly probable that Mary's first thought was that now everything was back to order. He wanted her to know that things would be different now; she couldn't hold on to the past. On the other hand, Mary may have been so fearful of Jesus "disappearing" again that she wanted to hold on to Him and never let Him go. Jesus reassured her that He wasn't going to vanish at any moment. He was not yet in the state of having ascended to the Father.

WORDS FROM WESLEY

John 20:16

It is the voice of my Beloved,
My fears are fled, my griefs removed,
He calls a sinner by his name,
And He is mine, and His I am!
Jesus by a word made known,
Thee my gracious Lord I own.
My gracious Lord I know, Thou art,
The lawful Master of my heart,
I feel Thy resurrection's power;
And joyful at Thy feet adore;
Now I only live to prove
Thou art God, and God is love. (PW, vol. 12, 104–105)

Jesus clearly revealed that His relationship with God was different from hers. He was returning to His and her Father. He didn't say "our Father," because Jesus stands in a unique relationship with Him. But notice that He called the disciples His **brothers** (John 20:17). Romans 8:29 tells us Jesus was the firstborn among many brothers, and Hebrews 2:11 says we "are of the same family. So Jesus is not ashamed to call them brothers."

Mary immediately obeyed the command of her Lord, relaying what she had seen and heard. Our primary responsibility as disciples of Christ is to tell the world what we have seen and heard—to share the good news of the gospel of Jesus Christ (see John 1:14; Acts 4:20; 10:39–43; 1 John 1:1–5; 4:14).

WORDS FROM WESLEY

John 20:17

But go immediately *to my brethren*—Thus does He intimate in the strongest manner the forgiveness of their fault, even without ever mentioning it. These exquisite touches, which every where abound in the evangelical writings, show how perfectly Christ knew our frame. *I ascend*—He anticipates it in His thoughts, and so speaks of it as a thing already present. To *my Father and your Father, to my God and your God*—This uncommon expression shows, that the only begotten Son has all kind of fellowship with God. And a fellowship with God the Father, some way resembling His own, He bestows upon His brethren. Yet He does not say, *Our God*: for no creature can be raised to an equality with Him: but *my God and your God*: intimating that the Father is His in a singular and incommunicable manner; and ours through Him, in such a kind as a creature is capable of. (ENNT)

It is interesting that Jesus appeared to Mary and sent her as a witness to the rest of the disciples. All of the angel appearances in connection with the resurrection were to women. In the first century, women had very few rights and even less credibility. In

---

a court of law, women were not considered credible witnesses and were not even allowed to testify. If the resurrection had been a fraud, the writers would have devised their stories with men as the witnesses to offer undeniable proof of Jesus' resurrection. But it wasn't a deception. The Son of God had risen from the dead and appeared to those who loved and worshiped Him.

The Purpose for John's Gospel (John 20:30–31)

Many scholars believe John's gospel originally ended with 20:30–31, and did not include chapter 21. Verses 30–31 sum up all John had been trying to teach through his account. Of the several words for *miracle* used in the Scriptures, John favored the word translated *sign*. All the miracles recorded were merely signs pointing to who Jesus really was (John 10:38; 14:11; Acts 2:22). Their primary purpose was not to impress onlookers with His power, but to attest to His Sonship and to prompt belief, thereby making abundant and eternal life a surety. The resurrection was the crowning miracle that authenticated Christ's deity. Paul said in Romans 1:4 that Jesus "was declared with power to be the Son of God by his resurrection from the dead: Jesus Christ our Lord." Jesus said, "But I, when I am lifted up from the earth, will draw all men to myself" (John 12:32). He came to offer himself as the atonement for humanity's sin and to bring us back to God. Every miracle, including the resurrection, gave proof of who He was (and is) and what He came to do. They were all meant to draw people to Christ and to prompt belief.

WORDS FROM WESLEY

John 20:31

But these things are written that ye may believe—That ye may be confirmed in believing. Faith cometh sometimes by reading; though ordinarily by *hearing*. (ENNT)

DISCUSSION

Although Jesus had predicted His resurrection, His disciples didn't anticipate that glorious event. Fear and sadness gripped them as Jesus' body lay in a tomb. As you read John 20:1–18, discover how the good news of Jesus' resurrection reached the disciples.

1. Why did Mary Magdalene and the other women (Luke 24:1) go to Jesus' tomb? *Anoint His body with spices — no small respect*

2. How do you explain Mary's reaction upon finding the tomb empty? *Shock* *Shows that Jesus had already left*

3. Read Matthew 28:2. What purpose do you believe was served by the angel rolling away the stone from the tomb? *Let people in*

4. Why did the arrangement of the strips of linen and the burial cloth cause John to believe Jesus had risen? *How they were arranged*

5. What did Mary think had happened to Jesus' body? What turned her despair into joy? *He had been taken — Jesus*

6. How does the fact that Jesus rose from the dead impact your attitudes? Your actions? Your hope?

7. At first glimpse of Jesus, Mary thought He was the gardener. Why do you think she made this misidentification? *She was disoriented and in shock*

8. Why did John record some of Jesus' miracles in his gospel? *To show who He was* *Not by them him.*

PRAYER

Hallelujah! Lord, You have overcome sin through the sacrifice of Jesus on the cross, and You have overcome death through His resurrection. Thank You, Lord, for giving all believers the victory through Jesus Christ!

WORDS FROM WESLEY WORKS CITED

ENNT: *Explanatory Notes upon the New Testament,* by John Wesley, M.A. Fourth American Edition. New York: J. Soule and T. Mason, for the Methodist Episcopal Church in the United States, 1818.

JCW: Wesley, C. (1849). *The Journal of the Rev. Charles Wesley.* (T. Jackson, Ed.) (Vol. 1–2). London: John Mason.

PW: *The Poetical Works of John and Charles Wesley.* Edited by D. D. G. Osborn. 13 vols. London: Wesleyan-Methodist Conference Office, 1868.

SCW: Wesley, Charles. *Sermons by the Late Rev. Charles Wesley.* London: Baldwin, Cradock, and Joy, 1816.

WJW: *The Works of John Wesley.* Third Edition, Complete and Unabridged. 14 vols. London: Wesleyan Methodist Book Room, 1872.

OTHER BOOKS IN THE
WESLEY BIBLE STUDIES SERIES

Genesis (available February 2015)
Exodus (available April 2015)
Leviticus through Deuteronomy (available June 2015)
Joshua through Ruth (available June 2015)
1 Samuel through 2 Chronicles (available February 2015)
Ezra through Esther (available April 2015)
Job through Song of Songs (available February 2015)
Isaiah (available April 2015)
Jeremiah through Daniel (available February 2015)
Hosea through Malachi (available June 2015)
Matthew
Mark
Luke (available September 2014)
John
Acts (available September 2014)
Romans (available June 2014)
1–2 Corinthians (available September 2014)
Galatians through Colossians and Philemon (available June 2014)
1–2 Thessalonians (available September 2014)
1 Timothy through Titus
Hebrews
James
1–2 Peter and Jude
1–3 John (available June 2014)
Revelation (available June 2014)

Now Available in the
Wesley Bible Studies Series

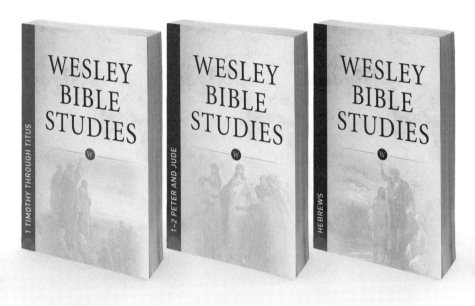

Each book in the Wesley Bible Studies series provides a thoughtful and powerful survey of key Scriptures in one or more biblical books. They combine accessible commentary from contemporary teachers, with relevantly highlighted direct quotes from the complete writings and life experiences of John Wesley, along with the poetry and hymns of his brother Charles. For each study, creative and engaging questions foster deeper fellowship and growth.

1 Timothy through Titus
978-0-89827-876-7
978-0-89827-877-4 (e-book)

Hebrews
978-0-89827-870-5
978-0-89827-871-2 (e-book)

1–2 Peter and Jude
978-0-89827-848-4
978-0-89827-849-1 (e-book)

wphonline.com
1.800.493.7539

CAUSEWAY

4 PRACTICE
4 4 ROUNDS

DUBLIN   Royal Portrush $200
         Royal County Down
         LAHINCH.

B&B.
         BALLYBUNION

Robert CAR